CULTURAL

DIVERSITY IN

LATIN AMERICAN

LITERATURE

CULTURAL DIVERSITY IN LATIN AMERICAN LITERATURE

D AVID W ILLIAM F OSTER

University of New Mexico Press
Albuquerque

Library of Congress Cataloging-in-Publication Data
Foster, David William.
Cultural diversity in Latin American literature / David William Foster. — 1st ed.
p. cm.
Includes bibliographical references (p.   ) and index.
Contents: Spanish American and Brazilian literature—Some proposals for the study of Latin American gay culture—Maria Elena Walsh : children's literature and the feminist voice—Argentine Jewish dramatists.
ISBN 0–8263–1490–2
1. Latin American literature—History and criticism. 2. Literature and society—Latin America. 3. Marginality, Social—Latin America. 4. Gays' writings, Latin American—History and criticism. 5. Children's literature, Latin American—History and criticism. 6. Feminism and literature—Latin America. 7. Argentine drama—Jewish authors—History and criticism. I. Title.
PQ7081.F628 1994
860.9'98—dc20   93–2459
CIP

Chapter 1 appeared in *Hispania* 75, no. 4 (1992): 966–78, a special issue commemorating the Columbus Quincentennial. Chapter 4 contains material that has appeared as "Four Argentine-Jewish Dramas of Cultural Conflict," *Modern Jewish Studies* 7, no. 4 (1990): 99–119; "*Krinksy* de Jorge Goldenberg y la étnica argentina," *Noah* 5 (1990): 51–54; *Latin American Theatre Review* 24, no. 2 (1991): 101–5; and "Argentine Jewish Dramatists: Aspects of a National Consciousness," *Folio* 17 (1987): 74–103; this chapter also includes a number of previously unpublished segments. The analysis in chapter 2 of Sara Levi Calderón's *Dos Mujeres* will appear in the proceedings of the University of Pennsylvania's Symposium on Contemporary Mexican Literature.

⋯⋙ CONTENTS ⋘⋯

Preface / *vii*

I
Spanish American and Brazilian Literature:
A History of Disconsonance / *1*

II
Some Proposals for the Study of Latin American
Gay Culture / *25*

III
María Elena Walsh:
Children's Literature and the Feminist Voice / *73*

IV
Argentine Jewish Dramatists: Aspects of a
National Consciousness / *95*

Conclusions / *151*

Notes / *157*

References / *165*

Index / *175*

⊷ PREFACE ⊶

The material brought together in this volume is to a large extent
the continuation of considerations that led me to publish *Alternate Voices in the Latin American Narrative* almost ten years ago:
the desire to move away from the insistent concentration of Latin
American literary criticism on a few authors, a few texts, and a few
problems, and to attempt to contribute to a reconfiguring of Latin
American cultural history. Many of the issues that only a decade
or so ago seemed so categorically on the scholarly margins have
now become major emphases. This is no more evident than with
testimonial writing and documentary narrative. On the one hand,
linked to feminist criticism (in which documentaries and testimoni-
als have bulked large in both the discovery of women's voices and
in the search for radically different discourse practices), such genres
bespeak the equally urgent need to confirm how Latin American
literature is much more than an echo of metropolitan traditions.
Feminist criticism, in spite of the application to Latin American
texts of American priorities and European theories, has brought
with it a large scope of considerations that revolve around concepts
such as the patriarchy, authoritarianism, gender-role tyranny, and
ethnic and racial hierarchies. My own response to this direction of
scholarly interests has led me to an examination of lesbian and gay
writing (both in terms of textual thematics and discourse ideologies)

and a parallel concern for Jewish identity with the (if only nominal) Christian hegemony of Latin America.

In not a totally different direction, Latin American scholarship has found it imperative to explore the boundaries not only of what can be considered literature but also of what the relationships are between a demarcated literary phenomenon and other cultural manifestations. Some of these manifestations may involve textual practices that overlap with literature strictu sensu, like the lyrics of songs or the scripts of movies and radio or television programs, whereas others may enter into more of a homologous than a literal relationship, such as when a film is treated as an integrated narrative on the same cultural plane, but in a different semiotic register, as the novel.

A different axis of this cluster of concerns involves the question of national literatures versus Latin American literature as a continental or Pan-American phenomenon. There are various ways to approach such an opposition, but whichever posture one assumes, it does not make much sense to continue to do so without recognizing the presence of Brazil as either the site of a national literature of the same category as any of the Spanish-speaking countries or as the source of important components for a totalized Latin American cultural production. The assimilation of Brazil as "just" another Latin American country is not at issue here. Rather, I suggest one must more properly be occupied with establishing something like a dialogic relationship between those literatures growing out of the Spanish language and those whose roots lie in a closely related language. It has always struck me as somewhat ironic that literary nationalism and regionalism has frequently promoted the integration of Spanish and indigenous languages, especially those that constitute major substrata for contemporary Latin American societies, but little attention is paid to the interconnections of virtually mutually intelligible languages such as Spanish and Portuguese. In fact, only the accidents of history have imposed the divergence of Iberian Romance into separate languages. (Obviously, Catalan is not involved here, because it never became a New World language, and I am assuming that the reader is familiar with how the designation *Spanish* itself is a convenient linguistic fiction for important dialect differences in the peninsula and their reflexes in Latin America.) Linguistic and cultural nationalisms may well have promoted divergences between Spanish and Portuguese in the New World, divergences that are probably greater than the difference between standard Portuguese and standard Spanish in the peninsula, as they have also promoted differences between different national standards of Latin American Spanish. But such circumstances cannot invalidate attempts to explore continuities between writing in Spanish and writing in Portuguese.

The chapters in this book do not constitute fragments for a new literary history of Latin American, less because they are so heterogenous than because it is now highly questionable what a literary history of Latin America might look like or even that one is theoretically possible and ideologically legitimate. By saying this, I do not mean to legitimate the mere assemblage of unrelated critical exercises. These texts are all related on the basis of one scholar's roaming around the Biblioteca de Babel that is Latin American culture, and they are all born of the enormously diverse interests that now characterize the very industrious house of Latin American literary scholarship. If there is any commonality, beyond the extent to which they are an index of unstable priorities, it is in the unabashed way in which they seek to validate an unguarded exposition of interpretive assertions. Rather than attempting to indulge in a fissureless argument that will be resistant to the objections of other informed opinions, I have sought to be (probably on more than one occasion, ingenuously) speculative, out of the belief that in these times a critical discourse about a culture that is urged to be marginal, dependent, and subaltern to one's own must necessarily speak with a voice whose problematic nature is all too evident.

Yet of course there is a unity to this material, imposed by a concern with the margins of critical discourse. The opening chapter is concerned with juxtaposing issues drawn from Spanish American and Brazilian writing. It is usually assumed that there is something like a continuum between the components of the former, based principally on what are now centuries-old debates on "the question of the Spanish language" and the common historical fact of the Spanish colonial empire; because Brazil speaks a different language (and acknowledging all of the arbitrariness over language boundaries) and had a different colonial history, its literary production is rarely interfaced with that of the Spanish American countries. I don't know if what is needed is a systematic review of the cultural production of five hundred years in the two regions of the continent, but Latin Americanists whose research is Spanish based cannot continue to pay only lip service to the existence of Brazil, if for no other reason than the simple fact that its literary history is stunning, and one avoids reading it at great loss. This chapter is only one of several projects that insists on normalizing, so to speak, the literary relations between Brazil and Spanish America and seeking ways to talk about the two areas without sounding superficially comparativist.

Chapter 2 reflects a continuing interest in discovering critical strategies for talking about lesbian and gay cultural production in Latin America, a research area that I first explored in *Gay and Lesbian Themes in Latin American Writing*. It seems to me that beyond the obvious imperative to free oneself from the descriptive mode (no small feat, as so much material remains simply to be identified and described in the realm of human experience routinely "hidden from history"), lies the need to explore protocols of analysis that avoid imposing on the texts a North American or European sociocultural agenda. To a certain extent this is inevitable, beginning with the very terms *lesbian* and *gay* and the political semantics they imply. It thus becomes not so much a question of freeing oneself from them as interacting with the implications of even using them in a critical discourse and of exploring ways to enrich them with specifically Latin American experiences, identities, and consciousnesses, without essentializing any of these categories in the process. Chapter 2 suggests some general conceptual considerations and then proceeds to discuss two novels, one by a man and one by a woman. The last segment of this chapter, in addition to pursuing the hypothesis that transgressive humor is one of the dominant options in Latin America for dealing with the sexual discourse so somberly theorized by the metropolis, proposes the need to examine documents that strain the conventional categories of literature—in this case, an autobiographical, but also presumably sociological, treatise, with its accompanying comic-book version.

There is no doubt that the bibliography of criticism on feminist topics has grown geometrically in recent years, and it is no longer possible to speak of women writers being ignored by the critical and academic establishments. Much work, to be sure, needs to be done. But there is no longer anything innovative in proposing a research program devoted to women writers framed along numerous distributive axes by period, nationality, class, race/ethnic origin, or thematics. Where there continues to be insufficient critical interest is in the area of children's writing, a topic I explored in *Alternate Voices* and to which I return with chapter 3, on the poetry and narrative of the Argentine *jongleur* María Elena Walsh. I am tempted to say that the bulk of feminist criticism has concentrated on writing by women that can compete in "seriousness" and artistic complexity with hegemonic writing by men, but such a statement would require the analysis of the terms themselves as highly problematical, especially in view of the influence in Hispanic criticism of Bakhtinian carnivalization in the context of the perceived need to question the high seriousness of literary production. But what I can say with the security of basing myself on objective bibliographic facts is that I know of no literary scholars with a research program devoted to the enormous presence in Latin American literature of writing for children by women and how that writing may or may not evince a feminist consciousness. The chapter included here suggests some ways in which this material may be approached.

By the same token, Latin American writing with an ethnic identity has experienced considerable recent attention, and there is a forthcoming volume of essays edited by Roberto Di Antonio and Nora Glickman devoted to Latin American Jewish writers. Naomi Lindstrom has published extensively on Argentine novelists and poets, and Di Antonio has authored important essays on Brazilian writers. Yet the record is spotty, and other groups—Arabs in Argentina, Chinese in Peru, and Japanese in Brazil come to mind—have hardly been addressed at all. What I have sought to do in chapter 4 is to explore Jewish issues as they are developed in a highly visible public spectacle such as the theater. Although there may be more of a novelistic production, and filmmaking in Argentina has always had a particularly prominent Jewish presence, theater is both a public genre and a high-culture format, and it is in this privileged cultural space that the concerns of the Jewish collectivity in Argentina were first given prominence in a fully national cultural discourse, and it is the uniqueness of the privilege and its specificity for one aspect of Latin American culture that make this chapter yet another example of framing underdeveloped zones of the critical analysis on Latin American literature.

In one sense these chapters provide a mosaic of concerns and emphases; in another, they suggest an alternate metaphor, that of a continuum of research projects that manifest dissatisfaction of uneasiness over anything that looks like the perpetual return to the same texts or the same topics. One understands the need constantly to revise, say, Borges in view of the often-heady developments in contemporary literary and cultural theory. There nevertheless must be a point at which other writers and other issues need to be addressed, not in the spirit of providing a balanced assessment of Latin American culture—one hardly knows what constitutes a balanced assessment or when it has been achieved—but in terms of recognizing that there is a broader production than criticism, especially in the United States, seems to suggest and that its importance and impact require assaying.

Throughout, the translations of the texts, unless otherwise indicated, are my own.

·⇌ I ⇌·

SPANISH AMERICAN
& BRAZILIAN LITERATURE:
A HISTORY OF DISCONSONANCE

Buenos Aires has traditionally seen itself, and been seen by others in
Latin America, as the cultural capital of the Spanish-speaking New
World. Mexicans, even Colombians and Peruvians, may not be particularly happy about this, but the fact remains that the Argentines
after independence (and particularly after ousting Rosas in the mid-
nineteenth century and after the capitalist bourgeoisie took over)
overcame their status as a colonial backwater by pursuing aggressively European cultural models that set the tone for the dominant
cultural elite in most corners of the continent.

This leadership role has never seemed to wane much, no matter how dictatorial regimes may strive to undermine the nation's
creativity—and foreign assimilationism—in the name of a closed
Catholic morality. Thus, one may find as a synecdoche of Argentine cosmopolitanism books in most of the major foreign languages:
wags might note that one can even find books in Spanish, although
non-Argentine authors are often hard to come by. There are bookstores specializing, of course, in books in English and French, and
the heritage of Italian and Jewish immigrants is honored by books in
Italian and Yiddish. The German ancestry of many immigrants before the war makes books available in that language, and, here and
there, one can find books in many other languages. Oriental immigration is the new wave in Argentina, and surely publications in Chinese, Japanese, Vietnamese, and so on are now available in the grocery stores these new arrivals have acquired along Corrientes in the
previously almost exclusively Jewish Once district of Buenos Aires.

But it is impossible to find books in Portuguese, and this in the largest Spanish American country to border Brazil. Newspaper kiosks in and around Calle Florida carry issues of O *jornal do Brasil* and *Manchete*, but the creatively designed volumes associated with Brazilian publishers are nowhere to be found in the dozens upon dozens of places one may scour for books in this very bookish city. Other aspects of Brazilian culture are just as rare—and an occasional Brazilian movie only underscores the general absence of Brazilian influence. The non-Spanish Americanism and lack of anything to remind them of home must certainly contribute to the foreignness that attracts Brazilian tourists to Argentina during the winter vacation period.

There is a fair degree of cultural interpenetration along the vast border Brazil shares with its Spanish-speaking neighbors, yet only the Uruguayans seem to have done anything with it the way of forging bicultural traditions. Of course, what is now Uruguay was once in Brazilian hands, and one of the country's historical reasons for being was to act as a buffer state between the two South American superpowers and archrivals. The principal centers of Brazilian culture are concentrated in a narrow strip along the eastern coast of the country (leading someone to remark once that, demographically speaking, Brazil is the Chile of the Atlantic coast), and the great distance between these centers and the capitals of contiguous countries has not been conducive to cultural symbiosis. The cultural center closest to a Spanish-speaking country is Curitiba, the agricultural and industrial capital of southern Brazil (it is the capital of the state of Paraná, which was heavily populated by non-Mediterranean immigrants), which is about five hundred miles from Asunción, the capital of Paraguay. But the "non-Brazilianness" of Paraná and Paraguay's long history of deadening dictatorships do not make for a promising inquiry into cultural exchange.

A very important sociocultural fact to bear in mind as one explanation of the lack of exchange between Brazil and Spanish America is how both countries have been engaged in the same pursuit of foreign cultural models in a way that excludes their having much to do with each other. In spite of Brazil's unique historical development, involving existence as an independent hereditary empire between its status as a Portuguese colony and the declaration of a constitutional republic, its dominant bourgeoisie has demonstrated the same trajectory as their counterparts in the bulk of the Spanish-speaking republics: a fascination consecutively, and overlappingly, with French, British, and American models in all facets of the life. This similarity, rather than the historical and sociological differences that might be postulated, accounts for the little contact between Brazil and Spanish-speaking America, at least of the sort that results in a production susceptible to comparative cultural analysis.

The historical and sociological differences spring immediately to mind. First, the aforementioned empire, whose sumptuousness competed with that of the Argentine nouveaux riches as an example of the Europeanized modern splendor capitalized wealth could amass. Second, there is language, although Spanish and Portuguese are so close that they should be called widely divergent dialects rather than separate languages. Certainly in the peninsula, the long coexistence of mutually intelligible Spanish and Portuguese dialects has led to much cultural exchange, despite the early definition of Portugal as politically independent from what would evolve into modern Spain.

Moreover, until the modernist[1] emphasis (beginning in the 1920s) on highlighting Brazil's linguistic independence from Portugal via the wholesale incorporation of indigenous foreign words and by the creolization of divergent structural features, academic Brazilian Portuguese did not look all that different from Spanish: most advanced Spanish majors have no difficulty reading Machado de Assis, although Mário de Andrade and João Guimarães Rosa may as well have written in Guarani, which they often seem to have done. But again, might not the similarities between the two languages explain why Brazilians rarely study Spanish and Spanish Americans, even less so, study Portuguese? Might there not be a belief that it is better to learn a truly foreign, prestigious language, such as French or English? The social pretentiousness and commercial interest that fostered the study of French and English in Latin America brought with it a respect for and for an assimilation of those cultures. And the mutual disinterest between the Spanish and Portuguese in the New World meant there would be little cultural intermingling.

Even possible coincidences in the area of black and indigenous culture come to naught. Although both the Spanish and the Portuguese imported black slaves, Brazil ended up with a more defined black and mulatto culture than did most of Spanish America. *Negritud* (a calque of French *négritude,* "blackness") has striven to correct the balance in Spanish America, but there is no equivalent for Brazil's black Bahia or strikingly integrated Carioca cultures, the Afro-Brazilian novels of Jorge Amado notwithstanding. (It should be mentioned that Amado is the one Brazilian writer widely read in Spanish, because his highly romanticized version of an exotic black culture ranges against a stereotypically racist white one.) It is doubtful that the evolution of something like "black pride" in Brazil ever found much to emulate in more racially oppressive Spanish America, or even in the Caribbean islands.

Although there is an anthropological continuity between the indigenous cultures of Paraguay and southern Brazil, the repression of the former by successive dictatorships and the dilution of the latter by German, Polish, Ukrainian, and other immigration result in insignificant traces of those indigenous cultures in most spheres. Conversely, the marginalization of the indigenous peoples by a society clinging to the Brazilian coast and the naïveté or disingenuousness of much of what has passed for "cosmic race" indigenism in Mexico and throughout the Andes mean equally disappointing bases for comparison. Mexico perhaps has done the best job of integrating indigenous elements into its culture, although its endeavor, which dates back to the programs derived from the revolution of 1910, is fraught with a certain degree of official myth-making vacuousness. Mexico's official indigenous policies are, nevertheless, far enough removed in space from the interest in Brazil sustained by anthropologists, linguists, and artists often in diametric opposition to government policies as to suggest few coincidences.

Literary language is at the heart of the most important movement in Brazilian culture in the twentieth century, one that is directly related to the international understanding of modernism. *Modernismo* in Brazil corresponds chronologically to its European equivalents, and, likewise, it has had a continuing projection in national literature and art, so much so that its hegemony has only in the last ten or fifteen years been shaken by an equally international postmodernism. Just as modernism made particular sense in the Brazil of the twenties, which was at least in the large metropolitan areas experiencing an expansive growth identified with a sense of the modern, postmodernism is afforded profound echoes by successive forms of institutional collapse in the country, the most recent being the evaporation of the promises of a return to a reasonable constitutional democracy and the solution to the country's staggering economic chaos. If modernism meant a faith in the definitive forging of a modern Brazilian self-identity as refracted by the manifestations of culture, postmodernism is a documentation of the breakdown of every aspect of the cultural and social codes.

What is impressive about modernism, however, is its initial vigor and its subsequent hardiness in the face of Brazilian sociocultural realities, even more so when one considers that its Spanish equivalent, *vanguardismo*, remains quite narrowly circumscribed in chronological terms, although the poetic career of certain of its principal figures, such as Pablo Neruda and Nicolás Guillén, extends far beyond the 1940 terminus ad quem. (It is necessary at this point to make the customary observation that Spanish American cultural historiography reserves the term *modernismo* for the Parnassian/symbolist aesthetic that dominates approximately between 1880 and 1920.) Spanish American modernism is generally seen as limited to a Mexico–Buenos Aires axis, crosscut by a second axis in the Andean region (César Vallejo in Peru and Neruda in Chile) and the Caribbean (largely by virtue of a Spanish-language version of *négritude* and the Cuban Orígenes group), and confined to the 1920s and 1930s. Brazilian modernism, by virtue of the tremendous cultural production associated with it in one national setting, seems by far the more coherent literary movement, and certainly the longer lived one. Yet it remains to be seen if a revisionist literary historiography will ultimately deconstruct Brazilian modernism and demonstrate that its much-vaunted successive phases constitute in reality profound discontinuities.

Certainly it is the preoccupation with the evolution of a truly national literary language that most provides the Brazilian modernist movement its coherency. Within the context of the international modernist commitment to art as the most essential form of human expression and to the construction of innovative stylistic forms to match the new, "modern" demands of knowledge and representation, Latin American modernism constituted a reprise of the continuing "question of language": the advisability and possibility of forging alternately continental (i.e., Pan-American) and national linguistic standards. It would be illusory to suggest that as the only Portuguese-speaking republic in Latin America, Brazil had it easier than the almost two dozen Spanish-speaking nations (leaving aside for this discussion the status of Francophone Haiti). By virtue of its enormous size and natural barriers, its radically different social history in the north, south, and center (even the differences between its two major points of reference, Rio de Janeiro and São Paulo), and the continuity of its demographically complex coastal strip versus the disjunction of its scattered centers of the interior, Brazil often seems to present linguistically and culturally as much social diversity as all the rest of Latin America. Thus concern for the development of a national linguistic norm, whether or not tied directly to modernism's most definitive expression in the urban intellectual and artistic circles of São Paulo, cannot avoid being viewed against the inevitably sustained fragmentation of Brazilian national culture.

Yet modernism did accompany the consciousness that a unifying national language was being achieved on both the literary and the colloquial levels. Indeed, one of the salient features of literary modernism was its ability to evoke a specifically literary dialect while defending colloquial registers, marginal sociolects (socially defined dialects, e.g., black speech), and even indigenous languages as reinvigorating donors to the national language. Modernism was very thorough in this, and the rupture on the literary level—and subsequently on the more conservative academic level—of the hegemony of peninsular Portuguese was far reaching. As was the case with the linguistic rupture with Spain during Spanish American *modernismo,* as a consequence of the belief that the mother country's culture had become hopelessly fossilized, the belief in Brazil that Portugal had fallen to a similar cultural nadir at the hands of reactionary leadership contributed to the opportunities afforded the international modernist mentality. Thus considerable changes in the national standard were effected by the literate elite's enthusiastic endorsement of phonologic (as reflected in a modernized orthography), morphosyntactic, and lexical features of colloquial speech; the massive incorporation of "futuristic" elements drawn from new prestige languages (such as English); and the "technocratization" of poetic language in general, whereby it was understood that artistic specialists, such as poets, would reshape the Brazilian Portuguese language to conform to the new social and cultural demands.

Undoubtedly, many of the same changes were taking place in Spanish during the same period, particularly if we bear in mind that some of the major Spanish-language exponents of modernism, such as Jorge Luis Borges (Argentina), Pablo Neruda, and César Vallejo, were moving in international circles that allowed them to see Spanish outside national and continental terms. (Borges's successive linguistic modalities have yet to be studied thoroughly in terms of his early commitment to German and his lifelong identification with English, particularly in the context of his repudiation of "rhetorical" Spanish both during and after his modernist enthusiasms.) Yet by the time of *vanguardismo,* Latin American Spanish had already sufficiently dissociated itself from peninsular norms so as to develop the characteristic national literary dialects that modernism only served to reinforce—so much so that linguistic nationalism often appears to be the only form of nationalism endorsed unequivocally from all points of the sociopolitical spectrum. The linguistic diversity of contemporary Spanish America is as much a consequence of modernism (though modernism was not its only impetus) as the palpable overlay of a national linguistic unity in Brazil, despite surviving regional differences.

Although in both Brazil and Spanish America, modernist ideology can be perceived in a form of linguistic consciousness and in the development of a wide diversity of national cultural forms that strive to substantiate the modernist belief in the cognitive and redemptive qualities of art, it is important to underscore how the fundamental instrument of modernism, internationally and in Latin America, was poetry. It vied with the emergence of realist and naturalist prose fiction during the latter decades of the nineteenth century and was the foremost testing ground of the modernist project, although early on modernism stimulated the development of an experimental narrative (compare the modernist novel *Macunaíma* [1928] by Brazil's Mário de Andrade and *Don Segundo Sombra* [1926] by Argentina's Ricardo Güiraldes).

Modernism, by stressing the centrality of language as part of the social dimension of its aesthetic program, reinstalled poetry as the highest form of linguistic expression, the most specialized form of linguistic discourse and the most malleable in the search for a correlation between expression and complex levels of experience. Poetry is both a primitive Ursprache and a highly specialized semiotic instrument of the modern world. It both bears the traces of the long, mythic development of societies and serves to chart the multiple evolutions of the present sociocultural consciousness. Because of its dense processes of signification, poetry is most able to provide the sense of the multidimensionality of modern man and to contribute to its continuing formation.

The many poetic manifestations associated with modernism in form, themes, voices, and pragmatic goals is a natural reflex of a full agenda specified by a heady allegiance to the power of poetic expression. The recovery of indigenous cultures, the revindication of popular motifs, the revision of the past, the mapping of all the diverse manifestations of the new urban culture, the reassessment of the rural within the purview of the urban, the stipulation of the relationships between the national and the international, the defense of specific political and social programs, and the by-no-means unambitious characterization of the importance of the individual poetic identity as the center of this vast process of signification: these are the major ventures of poets throughout Latin America—poets for whom the possibilities of poetic articulation go hand in hand with a sense of a modern Latin America that may now be in full possession of its own cultural, and therefore social and political, destiny. In the 1920s Buenos Aires and Mexico (modernism in Mexico acquired the added dimension of the nationalist cultural fervor in the wake of the 1910 revolution) were every bit as culturally dynamic as Rio or São Paulo, and even places like Havana and Santiago, Chile, were infused with the new consciousness following the Great War. Modernism in both these Spanish American centers and in

Brazil is a shared artistic and intellectual commitment because of modernism's international affiliations, despite the apparent lack of sustained contacts across the still-abiding abyss between Spanish and Portuguese.

Although there may have been a considerable number of Spanish American works from the narrative "boom" of the 1960s and 1970s translated into Portuguese—Juan Rulfo, Carlos Fuentes, Mario Vargas Llosa, Alejo Carpentier, Julio Cortázar, among others—few Brazilian works evincing the same or similar conceptions of fiction were translated into Spanish. Perhaps this oversight was the consequence of one central marketplace in the Spanish-speaking world; perhaps it is due to the way in which Argentine culture, Argentina being the logical place for such translations to be undertaken and published, systematically ignores Brazil. Whatever reasons might be alleged, the Spanish American and Brazilian contacts that existed in the narrative during this period tended to be one way, and this has continued to be the case into the 1990s.

One Brazilian writer who has achieved considerable currency among Spanish-language readers is João Guimarães Rosa. There are many reasons why Rosa is an important figure in Brazilian literature. First, there is his application of the most advanced conceptions of narrative prose to rural topics. By midcentury many believed that these topics had been sufficiently exhausted by a form of literary realism and local-color writing that dwelt insistently on the surface features of the various regional patterns of daily life in Brazil, features explored in terms of the prevailing social conflicts: class oppression, struggles between the city and the outback, and Western concepts of sophisticated living versus the continued adherence to primitive and archaic, but allegedly more authentic, practices and beliefs. Whereas Rosa continued to deal with many of these ideologemes, other contemporary writers wished to repudiate them in favor of the representation of the complexities of modern urban life. Moreover, in dealing with these subjects, Rosa used the arsenal of narrative strategies his contemporaries believed to be most suited for the characterization of a nonrural consciousness: fragmented and cyclical chronologies, split and refracted characters, multiple narrative ironies, a carnivalesque bricolage of events and dialogues, and the poetic foregrounding of a highly idiosyncratic language thoroughly at odds with the customary portrayal of rural speech.

Another reason for Rosa's popularity among Spanish-language readers is that he invested his characters with an inherent ideological deconstructionism that can counter the almost folkloristic typicalness of the dominant social fiction, as best represented in the charmingly superficial stereotypes of Jorge Amado's cast of Bahian figures. When Rosa has characters that initially appear to be textbook types becoming the focal point for heady issues of social philosophy such androgyny or polysexuality, or for the demythification of the alleged essentials of national character, he has created something radically different from the standard novel of social types and customs.

Finally, the very conception of a fluid and dynamic reality, the breaking down of the frontiers between "reality" and "fantasy" (concepts that must necessarily be bracketed when speaking of a world vision that begins by denying their conceptual validity), the attempt to chart forms of personal and collective experience that have not been—and, perhaps, cannot be—accounted for by existing means of representation, and the conviction that people may discover that what really constitutes a profound human experience lies beyond the ken of their received social codes: these all underscore the originality of Rosa's fiction.

Rosa's "third bank of the river" is the space beyond the ideologically frozen geography of daily social life, where the individual disembarks in the discovery of an existential reality beyond reality, where the absolute signifiers of an all-encompassing code are deconstructed in order to permit access to a profounder discourse. Beginning with the disarticulations of standard literary Brazilian Portuguese, Rosa pursues an aggressive campaign of misreadings of the basic cultural texts of his society in order to arouse a sense of alternate social meanings.

The Argentine writer Julio Cortázar is a striking example of someone working in Spanish with the same commitment to the productive misreadings of the social text. In one sense, Cortázar's literature is more versatile than Rosa's. Whereas Rosa exclusively wrote fiction, Cortázar complemented his novels and short stories with journalism, art history, poetry, and the speculative and mixed-media essay.

On the other hand, aside from some experimentations with the cacophony of the various national and social dialects of Spanish, particularly as they come together stridently among Latin American exile groups, Cortázar's major linguistic contribution was to write a very lucid and mildly ironic form of Argentine Spanish that, along with Borges's prose, confirmed a sort of official sophisticated norm for the language in that country.

Where one finds a firm coincidence between the two writers is in their shared commitment to the need to challenge rigid interpretations of a static and unquestioned social reality. This they pursue through the promotion of deconstructive readings of social and cultural myths in the case of Rosa, and through pseudopsychoanalytical readings of terror in the face of a mutable reality in the case of Cortázar. In both cases, the densely woven texture of worn and comfortable beliefs is gashed by happenings that are too urgent to be ignored while being unaccountable within the codes of conventional reality. Cortázar's *cronopios* and *famas* come up against the wall of prescribed reality, the latter rending to accept the iron bars of its signifiers, while the former blithely, but not always untragically, seek to bend them in their intuition that there are verdant fields of meaning beyond the prison house of language (language understood, of course, in its multiple manifestations beyond the immediately linguistic sense of the term). Alternately, Cortázar's characters settle themselves into the comfortable pockets of an absolutist (authoritarian) definition of experience, only to fall through the bottom into a realm of events that demand a new conception of the old values and explanations. Or his characters may stumble into a hopscotching that leads them over the edge into the void of a jumbling of all the codes of conventional but stultifying modes of existence. In all of these cases, the individual confronts with stunning suddenness a world of shifting meaning, a "model to be assembled," no matter what the personal and collective cost, in which life is lived in much more surprising and vital terms than held possible within the confines of the preconstructed reality of the polite, decent, bourgeois society Latin America wishes itself in large measure to be. For the sophisticated Europeans most Argentines like to see themselves as being, Cortázar's writing (from his Paris-based exile) promoted as much of a drift toward the third bank of the river as did

Rosa's within a Brazil committed to different but equally fettering social myths.

On quite a different axis, Guimarães Rosa evokes comparisons with the Mexican Juan Rulfo within the context of the literary representation of marginal, especially rural, social types. It has been thought that the most appropriate means of representing any social type in literature must involve the accurate depiction of his or her sociolinguistic register. If modern literature, as a high bourgeois cultural form, has defined a purportedly neutral written linguistic representation based on the standard, received sociolect of a dominant oligarchy that has in place an array of institutions to perpetuate its own self-image, classes or subclasses on the margins of the dominant group must face the problem of what their linguistic embodiment might be.

As against a neoclassic norm of linguistic homogeneity that either excludes or assimilates deviations, a folkloristic, indigenous, or creole impetus insists on a documentary, quasi-scientific respect for nonstandard registers. The problem has always lain, of course, in how to represent with the standard orthography and conventions marginal registers that have no orthography and are, in sociological terms, actually denied the status of an orthography. That is, the concept of a written language—and, therefore, of a written literature—evolves concomitantly with the dominant social classes for which written language is an instrument of power.

The romantic alternative and its derivations, evinced by the ultimately inconsequential attempts at orthographic reform by Sarmiento and others, was to adjust standard orthography to suggest the "flavor" of nonstandard speech. This alternative is still to be found in devices such as elision (*pa'allá* to represent one colloquial pronunciation of *para allá, esepción* for *excepción,* and so on) or regraphication (*ehto* for *esto, caye* for *calle*), which may or may not be accompanied by additional highlighting such as italic or boldface type. Although such an approach suggests the flavor of nonacademic or nonstandard pronunciation, it can hardly be associated with a scientifically based linguistic dialectology. That would demand a full phonetic transcription, which would be incomprehensible to the (academically) untrained. Because the likelihood of developing formal nonstandard orthographies is remote or simply incomprehensible, the problem of how to accurately record marginal speech with the conventional orthography and discourse structure remains essentially unresolvable.

The question writers came to ask themselves, however, is whether their goal should in fact be to leave a linguistically faithful record of rural, substandard, or nonacademic registers. Far from being a turning away from an interest in the "folk," such a reflection is concerned with the level of representation to be achieved. That is, where the tradition of oral folklore and its high culture projections in literature have stressed the accurate transcription of speech, Rulfo and Rosa are at the center of a contrary emphasis on the literary rewriting of levels of cognition, expression, and self-identification that are anterior to manifest utterances.

The emphasis on preverbal articulation implies a profound rift between the dynamics of cognition and the conventions of its representation. Because the former is preverbal (from a theoretical point of view, it is an open question whether it is prelinguistic, that is, whether or not cognition is circumscribed by the deep structures of language), linguistic representation is not the transcription of actual speech, to be assessed as accurate or inaccurate, as precise or broad. Rather, the representation of preverbal cognition can be nothing more than a complex and abstract algorithm, a hypothetical postulation proposed by a narrator who mediates between characters and readers. This mediation proceeds with a stylistic code that purports to be a laborious formulation of the structures of cognition and experience but is, nevertheless, essentially arbitrary it is configurations because it is in no way the transcription of linguistic utterances.

Therefore, the degree to which this representation adheres to conventional linguistic standards and the ways in which it deviates from them cannot be linked to a criterion of accurate sociolinguistic transcription. It is important to note that the texts of Rulfo and Rosa are often totally devoid of dialogue. Their characters do not speak, because, save for rigidly defined social circumstances, they live a life in which linguistic expression does not play a prominent role. What expression does take place is circumstantial, markedly phatic, and has little to do with the real issues of life the narrator is interested in exploring. These real issues take place or are perceived on a preverbal level of cognition, and their narrative depiction requires a structure of linguistic signs that involve neither sociolinguistic transcription nor conventional discourse. The dense prose of these writers, who are often described as using a complex and indirect free style, of representing a stream of consciousness, and of employing a host of strategies lumped under the designation of magical realism, is the attempt to develop a narrative language to probe the preverbal cognition of marginal social types. Whereas the early psychological novel, noted for its development of a stream-of-consciousness prose, was typically involved with representing individuals whose language registers were coextensive with those being used by their narrators, Rulfo's and Rosa's characters are likely to neither belong to the linguistic realm of the readers (i.e., individuals trained in both the conventions of academic prose and high culture literature) nor to manipulate the semiotics of their narrators. To the extent that the narrators have developed a complex code of linguistic and narrative representation for the readers' specific and preverbal forms of cognition and sentience, the result is a linguistic and narrative texture that exploits all of the experimentation of modernist writing (along with the projections of postmodernist deconstruction and disruption) in the name of the literary rewriting of marginal social types.

Although both Rulfo and Rosa may continue to make abundant use of a colloquial and rural vocabulary, and even some details of a nonacademic morphosyntax, their prose is a far cry from the folkloristic registers of the romantic, creole, and indigenous traditions. Like Peru's José María Arguedas, Paraguay's Augusto Roa Bastos, or Cuba's Severo Sarduy, Rulfo and Rosa understand that what needs to be represented is not overt speech, but multiple levels of preverbal expression that are not tied to any one sociolinguistic register or even to any one language. The narrative semiotic that results from this conviction uses linguistic structure not as a tool for the transcription of speech, but as a highly supple and inventive instrument for exploring the ways in which to display a "deep level" perception of personal and social experience. Such an exploration becomes, in turn, a cultural form of mediation between individuals viewed as being on the margins of, and systematically excluded from, the dominant social power and that social power in the form of a coextensive cultural modality—literature and literary language.

Rulfo and Rosa wield highly complex forms of literary discourse for the representation of marginal social types while they seek to validate the personal and collective stature of marginal characters through a dense narrative image of their processes of cognition and sentience. The fundamentally modernist commitment to the possibility of developing a complex, expressive language for the depiction of marginal individuals deprived of socially acceptable linguistic registers or confined to an insignificant phatic speech viewed as "charming" and ingenuously humble is a significant similarity between writers like Rulfo and Rosa.

Feminism, like countercultural identities, is, in one prevailing Western view, widely endorsed by Latin American intellectuals, essentially a matter of sociopolitical reality that affects everyone, not just feminists. Moreover, because feminist writing shares with literature on lesbians and gays an exploration of the tensions of the social text as they impinge on individual liberties in the form of authoritarianism, repression, and persecution, it often reveals some of the most original and audacious creativity in contemporary culture. The inventory of women writers in Latin America, specifically feminist or otherwise, and new as well as hitherto-ignored or forgotten names, has become impressive indeed.

The inevitable point of reference for any discussion of women writers in Brazil is Clarice Lispector, a writer whose fiction has achieved as much international recognition as that of Machado de Assis and João Guimarães Rosa. Before feminism came to the fore as a necessary optic for treating both the male and female characters of women authors, Lispector's novels and short stories were apt to be discussed as exemplars of the generally existentialist posture that held sway at the time of her first major works. Her narrative world is populated with individuals who are obsessively self-contemplative, and her combined interior monologue and dense authorial commentary results in a complex analysis of motivations, feelings, and consequences of the most minute or trivial of human actions. When seen from a feminist perspective, these actions focus themselves sharply as the reflexes of painfully sentient men and women trapped in the labyrinth of social and moral conventions.

Although her characters cannot successfully free themselves from convention, through either ultimately feeble actions or excruciating convolutions of self-scrutiny, as narratives, Lispector's texts become telling deconstructions of the prevailing codes of our world. The very commonness of her men and women make the analyses of the narrative voices and their own self-examinations all that more eloquent as a discourse on the collision between the material texture of daily life and the cruelly empty illusions of transcendence propagated by the controlling ideologies of politics, religion, and culture. Lispector, as a feminist writer, is certainly in the deconstructionist mode, which antedates the currently more prevalent ethic whereby writers have the obligation to provide their readers with images of marginal individuals who are able to triumph and transcend despite the repressive structures of convention and oppressive structures of political containment. Severely unromantic writers like Lispector and Lygia Fagundes Telles, a novelist who covers much the same ground but with an emphasis on dialogue between her characters rather than on an often-leaden interior monologue of the sort Lispector strives to achieve, might well feel that portrayals of ideological victories for feminism, gay rights, or ethnic identities are jejunely American.

The feminist restructuring of the canon has brought into focus the clear importance of writers like Chile's María Luisa Bombal and Marta Brunet for their echoes of the type of feminist analysis associated with Lispector—an analysis, it must be stressed, that does not deal exclusively with female characters, but involves representations of male characters beyond the restrictive heroic/tragic (and occasionally comic) dimensions of patriarchal conventions. Authors like Bombal, Brunet, Lispector, Telles, literary feminists *avent la lettre,* are of crucial importance in obliging the literary historian to establish a tradition of exopatriarchal writing in Latin America, or even to consider the problematic issue of nineteenth-century women writers who may have attempted to assimilate their writing into a version of the patriarchy. Clorinda Matto de Turner is of interest in this regard, just as Argentina's Juana Manuela Gorriti is so strikingly against the grain. When one considers the hegemony achieved by the liberal, patriarchal oligarchy throughout Latin America—at least in those countries usually claimed to have been in the cultural vanguard—it is not surprising to find an almost total absence of feminine voices. It is only with the breakdown of this tradition beginning in the 1930s that women writers come to the fore, which only makes precursors such as Uruguay's late symbolist, but highly erotic, poet Delmira Agustini (who was allegedly shot to death by her husband as immoral) all the more exceptional.

It would seem that despite Brazil's recent efforts on behalf of women's rights and impressive openness to the incorporation of women in positions of professional and public influence, Spanish-language women authors have been more audaciously innovative than their Brazilian counterparts. One cannot readily determine Brazilian parallels to the versions of eroticized female consciousness of Puerto Rico's Rosario Ferré, the journalistic and documentary writings of Mexico's Elena Poniatowska, the political interpretations of female experience of Argentina's Marta Lynch, or the unrelenting dissection of crushingly destructive patriarchal authority of Argentina's Griselda Gambaro.

Brazil, like Argentina and other neighboring countries, experienced a particularly Draconian form of military tyranny in the 1960s and 1970s. Lynch's novels, among them *La penúltima versión de la Colorada Villanueva* (1979) and *Informe bajo llave*, (1983) are notable for their exploration of the impact of this dominant strain of patriarchal authoritarianism on feminine—if not specifically feminist—consciousness. Her characters exist in a dangerous relationship to authoritarianism, dangerous because of the suffering in the world around them they sense as deriving directly from it and dangerous because of the punitive consequences that flow from challenging authoritarianism, no matter how timidly and tentatively, in thought and action. The idea of women caught in a double bind of emotional and physical anguish because of, first, their awakening to their marginal role in society and, then, the suffering, and often literal torture and death, that descends on them for challenging that role constitutes a sustaining postulate for a good amount of feminist writing in Latin America.

Because the consequences of challenging authority in authoritarian societies are usually more explicitly dreadful, as opposed to the greater psychological repercussions in allegedly democratic "open" societies, writers such as Lynch and Gambaro have much to say about the material consequences of the several successive stages of attempts at liberation. Moreover, Gambaro is one of Latin America's most successful dramatists. In the case of one segment of her writing, the representation of the dynamic of oppression is vividly graphic, resulting in a very Latin American version of a theater of cruelty, both in the cruelty toward human dignity of the social structures dealt with and in the cruelty of the relentless theatrical assault on the complacency of the spectator. Ferré, writing within a Hispanic enclave of American society, is less faced with the issue of overt tyranny. Yet Puerto Rican society may be seen as a caricature of WASP respectability, and the eroticization of Ferré's characters (a quality that is still to be found only sporadically among Latin American women writers; see, however, the brilliant treatment of female sexuality by Mexico's María Luisa Mendoza in her novel *De Ausencia* [Concerning Ausencia; 1974]) is an impressive repudiation of desexualization on the grounds of moral principles sustained by the conventional feminine ideal. The disingenuous vacuousness of this ideal as promoted through masculine interests and acquiesced to by passive women was challenged early on in contemporary Latin American society by Mexico's Rosario Castellanos and Argentina's Silvina Bullrich. The eroticization of the female body and its sociopolitical consequences, however, constitute important advances in the feminist liberation from the patriarchal definitions of both male and female sex.

Poniatowska is at the center of the development of a documentary narrative because she wishes to not only deal with specifically feminist issues but also lay bare the deep rifts of Mexican society covered by layers of official hypocrisy. The overriding preoccupation with the nature of power and its various forms of official and countercultural discourse is understandably at the heart of a feminist imperative to deconstruct sociopolitical institutions, to engage in a radically revisionist public history, and to rewrite the parameters for the participation of the individual, man or woman, in the national power structure. In effect, her most famous works, *La noche de Tlatelolco* (Massacre in Mexico; 1971) and *Hasta no verte Jesús mío* (See You Around, Sweet Jesus; 1969), for example, involve an artful combination of documentary modes: sophisticated investigative reporting; representations of specific women's issues, such as the recovery of lost or marginal participants in history (the *soldadera* [camp follower] is allowed to tell her own story in *Hasta no verte Jesús mio*); and the elucidation of the patterns of individual and collective consciousness about the nature of events official history would ignore or explain away, as in the polyphonic chorus of outrage over the student massacres immediately preceding the 1968 Olympic Games (in *La noche de Tlatelolco*).

The result of these documentary narratives has been an enormous amount of enthusiasm for Poniatowska's works as exemplars in Latin America of a balance between intersecting political and feminist concerns. Although Brazilian literature reveals some examples of documentary narrative, particularly Miguel Jorge's and José Louzeiro's various texts on criminal cases—*Aracelli meu amor* (Aracelli, My Love; 1976) and *Lúcio Flávio, o passageiro da agonia* (Lúcio Flávio, or Agony's Child; 1975) are Louzeiro's most famous, the former made into a successful play and the latter into a movie by the Argentine director Héctor Babenco—there are yet no outstanding women's voices exploring the advantages of documentary modes for the promotion of feminism and/or sociopolitical interpretation. One is left with the impression that after Lispector's innovative fictional analyses of consciousness, the majority of Brazilian women writers have been content to manipulate, with equally impressive results, the modalities preferred by their more-touted masculine counterparts.

Brazilian writers reveal a sustained commitment to science fiction, particularly as a dimension of social criticism. If one subscribes to the thesis that science fiction is less a projection of enthusiasm over technology than it is a reaction to it, it is understandable that Brazil, a continent-sized country with a population concentrated in urban areas characterized by an almost patriotic fascination with technological development, shows an interest in science fiction, in both the translation of foreign authors and local production. By contrast, neither Mexico nor Argentina, the two most industrialized countries of Spanish America, have much of Brazil's mythified interest in technology. As a consequence, whereas Brazilian literature has a sustained science fiction subgenre, Spanish American literature has only sporadic examples, and most of these are quite mediocre by international standards.

It is ironic that the film *Brazil*, on the fascist uses of technology as epitomized in a Western European industrial setting, proffers the image of Brazil as a libido-releasing escape from oppression. Despite the international image of an uninhibited society, as extrapolated from the tourist's understanding of carnival, Brazil has hardly been mistaken by Brazilians themselves as a nonrepressive, oppression-free society, at least since the Brazilian version of the fascist movement beginning in the 1930s. Increasingly, technology developed in Europe and the United States for the control of the individual has been used by Brazilian authoritarian regimes, allowing for the abundant appearance in contemporary Brazilian writing of science fiction narremes of the disastrous consequences of the unchecked technological abuses of the environment and the deployment of specialized technical instruments to control, persecute, and "correct" the citizenry.

The novel *Não verás país nenhum* (1982) by Ignácio Luis Brandão, which was translated into English as *And Still the Earth* and included in Avon Books' Latin American series, is an excellent example of the adaptation of a science fiction perspective to charting the fault lines of contemporary Brazilian society. The appalling living conditions resulting from uncontrolled expansion, the breakdown of social and sanitary services, the oppression that comes from the need to restrict severely a populace alternately zombified and on the brink of rebelling, and the breakdown of the sense of human community that makes life bearable are all motifs elaborated by Brandão in his novel about a futuristic São Paulo that, colored more starkly, has been understood by readers to be the one now at hand.

Because science fiction counters the unreflective paeans to technology and science with sobering analyses of the destruction of the individual that science is able to bring about in geometrically expanding waves of horror, Brazilian novelists have undoubtedly felt that their writing must serve to call attention to the nature of oppression in their society by examining one of the mechanisms that in the modern age has served to keep oppression in place and that will function to increase it in the future. In addition to Brandão, André Carneiro, Ruth Bueno, José Gilberto Noll, and Rubem Fonseca are also worth noting in this regard.

The other subject that in Brazilian writing has only sporadic confluences with Spanish American texts is homosexuality. Although Latin American fiction in general reveals intermittent references to homosexuality as a tragically regrettable feature of the hidden recesses of the human psyche (e.g., the Chilean Augusto D'Halmar's *La pasión y muerte del cura Deusto* [Passion and Death of Father Deusto; 1924]) or as a sexual trace of a degraded and/or corrupt character (e.g., the Argentine Roberto Arlt's *El juguete rabioso* [The Rabid Toy; 1926]), only in Brazil is there a large body of writing that accepts homosexuality as a reasonable social component that demands understanding and protection. Although the tragic mode continues to dominate—tragic because either such love is viewed as inherently doomed or social prejudice and persecution makes it an impossible form of human fulfillment—Brazilian literature reveals an impressive inventory of treatments of the subject, reaching back to Adolfo Caminha's *Bom Crioulo* (The Good Nigger; 1895 [the published English translation retains the original Portuguese title]), perhaps one of the earliest explicitly gay novels in Western literature. The first of Leyland Winston's two volumes of English translations of gay Latin American texts contains so much Brazilian material that the Library of Congress has classified it as an anthology of Brazilian writers, and the texts contained in both volumes constitute coverage of all the principal chronological periods of Brazilian literature. By contrast, despite explicitly gay texts by a number of contemporary Spanish American writers—Oscar Hermes Villordo in Argentina, Isaac Chocrón in Venezuela, José Joaquín Blanco and Luis Zapata in Mexico, and Jorge Marchant Lazcano in Chile—it is difficult to establish specifically gay texts over a chronological range of writing in Spanish, either nationally or continentally (note, however, that one fascinating potentially gay text is the famous, and maddeningly ambiguous, short story "El hombre que parecía un caballo" [1915] by Guatemala's José Arévalo Martínez).

In Mexico, the emphasis of gay writers such as Zapata and Blanco has been on contrasting the patriarchal, Christian family-unit image of a heterosexual dominant society with the inevitable complexities of human relationships that arise in expanding urban societies, along with the need to explore alternate forms of bonding and fulfillment. Characteristically, the hypocrisy of bourgeois culture emerges in the clash between the ideals of boy-girl romantic love and the impossibility of complying with such an ideal in a fragmented and alienating environment. Homosexual relationships are not necessarily seen as any better in dystopian Mexico—indeed, Zapata runs the risk with a novel like *En jirones* (In Shreds; 1985) of being accused of lingering homophobia because his protagonists end up so battered. But the point of focusing on them is to bring out the ways in which contemporary Mexican lives are much more variegated and complex than middle-class publicity leads one to believe.

Writers such as Manuel Puig and Villordo come close to the Brazilian emphasis on the direct political dimension of homosexuality by combining the continuities between political liberties and sexual freedom. If their protagonists continue to fare badly, both despite and because of sexual preference and a so-called alternate life-style, it is because the dominant structures they are challenging are too rigidly oppressive to permit them their personal liberty. Thus the point of the narrative is to underscore the resulting social dissonance of this circumstance and the suffering and destruction of the individual that it produces. That the issue of sexual freedom is contained within the problem of personal liberties as a whole in authoritarian societies makes homosexuality a synecdoche of human rights. It serves in a particularly dramatic way, because of how it continues to discomfit society, to highlight the dynamics of repression and its complement, persecution. This is brought out very well in the aforementioned Argentine novels and, in Brazil, in a text such as Aguinaldo Silva's *No país das sombras* (1979), in which the postulation of a history of gay persecution suggests the incorporation of homophobia into the founding of Brazilian society.

Silva's novel is an attempt to understand the conditions of the homosexual experience within the larger context of Brazilian social reality. Two basic narrative axes emerge: a homosexual "crime" as metonymic of a founding act of social repression and the typological echoes that exist between contemporary political experience and successive historical events. The narrator, a journalist and historical researcher who stumbles upon an obscure event in early Brazilian colonial history that comes to assume for him the proportions of a master scheme, ultimately reaches the conclusion that the only purpose of the past is to explain the present in order to modify it. Written against the backdrop of violent acts of social repression, the narrator's text unfortunately, is unable to do much to modify the present, and at the end of the novel, the narrator becomes one more victim of police brutality.

Silva frames his novel as an exercise in historical research that will reveal the expanding synecdochic relationship between founding acts of violence and an abiding social code based on the hypocritical justification of repression and the cynical justification of social and political dissidence. Specifically, *No país das sombras* deals with two young soldiers who, during the first decades of the Portuguese occupation of the New World, enter into a homosexual relationship. One of them, however, is the object of desire of the chief of the military garrison, who harbors a pedophilic interest behind the facade of his proper marriage and social rectitude. Determined to separate the man he desires from his lover, the *general-provedor* informs them that they will be posted to separate stations. Rather than accept this separation, the two men lure the general-provedor to a secluded spot and murder him. Seen leaving the jungle area where the body is later discovered, the two men are arrested, accused of murdering their officer as part of a plot to revolt against Portuguese rule, tortured to extract a confession to this effect, and hanged. Although the majority of the scarce remaining documents echo the allegations of sedition, Silva's narrator is able to ferret out an alternate reading of history in which the official explanation is a smoke screen for a tawdry episode involving sexual jealousy and revenge—and, of course, cynical official hypocrisy.

Silva's novel enjoys an inverted intertextuality with the utopian feelings of colonial chronicles of the Conquest that saw the New World as the opportunity to fulfill the Renaissance ideals of European culture. The executed lovers are the victims of a dystopian repression that punishes them for both their outlawed sexual behavior and the energy of social revolt it engenders. As a founding act of Brazilian social history, the homophobic persecution of the soldiers the narrator rediscovers in his research installs a dynamic of social repression to which the narrator himself, more than three hundred years later, inevitably falls victim. The importance of a novel such as Silva's is that, like Puig's *El beso de la mujer araña* (Kiss of the Spider Woman; 1976), which frames explicitly the conjunction of fictional narrative and sociological thought, the conflict between personal liberty and political repression is foregrounded so vividly within the context of a specific reading of the sociohistorical text.

This chapter hardly represent a formally comparativist examination of the relationships between Brazilian and Spanish American literature. Rather, it constitutes primarily an inventory of the most salient manifestations of contemporary writing in Latin America, with observations regarding the continuities and discontinuities between Brazilian authors and their Spanish-language colleagues. It also underscores what I consider to be the most interesting aspects, because most innovative and challenging to readers who may prefer the conventionalized varieties of literary discourse, of twentieth-century literature. In the latter sense, this chapter cannot even be considered a balanced inventory of all the basic forms poetry and narrative have taken on either or both sides of the Spanish-Portuguese language frontier. At best, it can help to stimulate the more rigorous forms of comparative literary analysis between Brazil and Spanish America that have been so notably lacking in our literary historiography. In turn, such studies ought to contribute to a necessary symbiosis between the two major blocks of Latin American writing and culture, so vital to a more properly grounded continental consciousness, than yet exists.

II

SOME PROPOSALS FOR
THE STUDY OF
LATIN AMERICAN GAY CULTURE

> Gay writers have not generally tried to create their own
> mythology independent of the heterosexual world; rather in
> the last three hundred years, they have sought to modify the
> sexual terms they have received, inscribing less a "reverse
> discourse" of homosexuality, than a subdominant one, a
> transcription of the original into a distant, unrelated key. . . .
> Since homosexuals have fashioned their sense of themselves
> out of and in response to the heterosexual discourse about
> them, homosexuality—even as conceived by homosexuals—
> cannot be viewed outside of the constructs of heterosexuality.
>
> —Bergman

This chapter is guided principally by a constructionist, nonessential-
ist view of homosexuality, with the necessary implication that one
cannot speak diachronically of a unified homosexual phenomenon
nor synchronically of a unified set of experiences across contemporary cultures. This is so whether one speaks of homosexuality in
terms of sex acts, sexual identity, or behavior traits, because from
this conceptual frame of reference, acts, identity, and behavior traits
only exist as the consequence of ideological definition, with ideology being understood as circumscribed by a cluster of social axes or
parameters that are not in any meaningful way reduplicated from
one time or place to another.

If one can contemplate the probability that the discussion of homosexuality, in whatever definition(s) one chooses to assign to it, loses sociocultural specificity to the degree that it is generalized outward from a limited but nevertheless hegemonic frame of reference such as Western Europe or the United States, one ought also to consider the very serious problems associated with attempting to generalize with respect to a vague concept like "Latin America." There can be no question that sexual identity varies enormously in all sorts of sociocultural dimensions within the hegemonic definitions that reign in the dominant-languages bibliography, and a significant portion of a responsible research agenda has been to pursue variations according to racial, ethnic, and class distinctions; gender differences, although not always going without saying, at least in primitive formulations, are taken as being beyond the specific male-oriented purview of the present exposition. The profound discontinuity between English-speaking and other dominant-language discussions on the one hand and subaltern (or, from the hegemonic societies' point of view, subalternized) identities on the other both overlooks substantive differences regarding the conceptualization of homosexuality and promotes in the subaltern a self-consideration that may be either positively or negatively charged. In the former case, the message is that we have something different to show you, whereas in the latter, it is that, regretfully, we lag significantly behind you in dealing with these matters.

Research in a society like the United States can now examine, without the need to uniformize, the substantial differences in gay identity along all sorts of multiple social axes. This is certainly the result of the shift in emphasis away from the concept of homosexuality as a group of deplorable acts to be dealt with in judicial, religious, or social-custom terms and toward research formulations that seek to understand how homosexuality, with or without specific acts, interfaces with other ideologically defined social behaviors, and, most intriguingly, how homosexuality may be part of an economy of psychosexuality whereby it performs an integral function within the social dynamic: Native American berdache clans, (semi)legal homosexual prostitution, masculine-affirming gay bashing, *cavalieri serventi* and so on.

Not only is Latin America not the United States or Western Europe, despite all of the propaganda regarding how the Columbus encounter brought to the New World the blessings of Western culture (which would include the Reformation and Counter-Reformation definition of homosexuality that enabled the vigorous campaigns against the sodomy found or imagined in indigenous societies), but Latin America is, of course, a cluster of many different societies whose one absolute commonality is confinement within a geographically determined space.

Although there can be no denying common origins, there are important ways in which continuities and discontinuities may be established. For example, from one point of view, by the same token that all dialects of Spanish are mutually intelligible, Spanish and Portuguese are closely related on a continuum of Iberian Romance, neo-Latin languages, and in many social circumstances (typically, noncolloquial, nonintimate settings) speakers of the two languages can converse with one another quite satisfactorily. Yet from another point of view, nationalistic pressures for cultural differentiation have fomented a sense of difference not only between Spanish and Portuguese but also between national dialects of Latin American Spanish, a phenomenon that also extends to difference in regional dialects within large countries such as Argentina, Mexico, Colombia, and, to be sure, Brazil. These differences involve components of internal influence, drawn typically from pre-Columbian indigenous languages and external lexical influence, deriving typically from immigrant languages such as Italian, Yiddish, and Japanese and dominant foreign languages such as English and French. They may also involve basic linguistic components such as phonology and morphosyntax. The point here is that linguistic identity is very much a synecdoche of large-scale questions of sociocultural and historic national identity and of the ways in which sociological questions, such as sexual identity, may be differentiated from one country to another.

For example, there is much to be learned by the way in which the closely tied neofascist military dictatorships in Argentina during the 1970s and 1980s and the Pinochet dictatorship in Chile during the same period dealt with the question of homosexuality. One significant commonality between the Latin American republics is the fact that homosexual acts are, generally speaking, not criminalized by constitution or legal code. This is the consequence of the combined influence of the Napoleonic legal system adopted throughout Latin America during the period of independence (1810–30) and subsequent national formation in the nineteenth century, with the exception of the different destinies of Brazil, Cuba, and Puerto Rico (although Brazil later followed the pattern of the rest of Latin America); Puerto Rico, of course, is consigned to the legal orbit of the United States. It also involves an essential, yet not universal, repudiation of Spanish Counter-Reformation Catholicism. Thus although the Catholic tradition continues to denounce homosexuality (along, to be sure, with a lush garden of other sexual miscreancies) and exercise (in conjunction with other religions, such as Judaism and, more recently, Mormonism) an enormous influence in creating a societal disposition against homosexuality, homosexual acts are not in themselves criminal.

Public indecency may be prosecuted (a proviso that has often hampered the public display of gay culture in the form of cruising, bars, festivals, demonstrations, and the like) and laws against the corruption of minors stringently enforced (a powerful tool for social control, of course, in the educational system and in cultural production in general), yet homosexuality as such, whether viewed as (primarily) acts or as an identity, is not criminal in Latin America. This is why in Manuel Puig's novel *El beso de la mujer araña* (Kiss of the Spider Woman; 1976) and Héctor Babenco's film version of it (with the English title), Molina is incarcerated for the corruption of a minor, not for any of the other homosexual transgressions that can bring prosecution in the United States (cf. Foster, *Contemporary Argentine Cinema* 123–35 concerning the codes of homosexuality in Babenco's film). Needless to say, wherever the law enforcement or judicial system is corrupt, constitutional guarantees and statutory exclusions are meaningless, and definitions of the corruption of minors may be interpreted in many and creative ways in order to abet persecution: legend has it that one colonial judicial authority explained his blatant exercise of arbitrary authority by affirming "the King is in Spain, God is in Heaven, but *I* am right here."

Which leads us to the question of military authority during periods of the suspension of constitutional protections. In Argentina, as in many other parts of Latin America where the armed services have suspended the constitution "in order to protect it" in the name of vague concepts like national security and sovereignty, government based on military authority has brought with it the persecution of homosexuality as, first and foremost, a question of soldierly discipline. The antilogy, if not the hypocrisy, of homosexuality within the context of the male-bonding necessarily promoted by a homosocial military service are too familiar to require rehearsing here. Military discipline, Catholic morality, and the traditional family unit, which are the components of society customarily supporting reactionary or neofascist regimes, have joined hands, with the result that sexual morality becomes quite narrowly defined. Such definitions echo and, at least in the early stages after a coup, receive the general endorsement of dominant homophobic public opinion. Consequently, homosexuals are lumped with a wide range of persecuted elements—alleged subversives and revolutionaries, free-speech advocates, intellectuals, creative voices, and social dissidents in general—all defined in ways that escape the troublesome precision of the legal code.

Whether military authorities view homosexuals as challenging the masculist authority of the armed forces, as one can find in fictional images in novels by the Peruvian Mario Vargas Llosa or the Argentine David Viñas, or as dramatically symptomatic of the social diseases the coup is meant to remedy—and these are really only two sides to the same ideological coin—gays have always had a rough time in Latin America under military rule, whether late nineteenth-century and early twentieth-century regimes of the Somoza variety or more recent neofascist and corporatist regimes of the Pinochet variety. One must, moreover, bear in mind that this scheme of things is just as applicable to the military authority of other political ideologies: no one need entertain any illusions about homosexual rights in socialist Cuba, where Castro's infamous persecution of gays and lesbians is far from an aberration of the revolution, far from merely the reaction to the bourgeois corruption that saw Havana as one enormous capitalist brothel (the perfect counterimage to, and escape valve for, Ozzie and Harriet's Eisenhower-years America). Rather, it is undoubtedly an integral part of the militarism, with all the homophobia of that tradition and its old-line socialist priorities (including the denunciation of homosexuality as bourgeois decadence), that has sustained the Stalinist Castro government. The persecutions described in the documentary film *Conducta impropia* (Improper Conduct) and the concentration camps that are the backdrop of Reinaldo Arenas's *Arturo, la estrella más brillante* (Arturo, the Brightest Star; [1984]) may no longer be the order of the day in Cuba, but the revolution has yet to do anything on behalf of gay rights.

But whereas the military juntas in Argentina, a country with a long tradition of conservative and often reactionary Catholic influence, vigorously persecuted gays and repressed gay culture as part of the correction of any manifestation of social dissidence, Pinochet, although he may have subscribed to all of the homophobia to which his Bismarkian heritage entitled him, did not view homosexuals as a significant threat to the authority of his nationalistic reconstruction of Chilean society. Santiago has always had a prominent Bohemian tradition, not only in the Wildean sense of otiose upper middle–class enfants terribles but also with significant parallel proletarian manifestations likely to be most noticeable in a wide-open port city like Valparaíso, especially in the heyday of international shipping. Valparaíso belongs to a constellation of dockside-culture port cities in Latin America—including Buenos Aires, Montevideo, Cuzco, Rio de Janeiro, and Veracruz—that have been legendary for prostitution. One cannot say that gay culture prospered under Pinochet, although a case, as always, can be made for the protection of establishment gays who supported the dictatorship. But homosexuals in Chile did not suffer as a group the sort of persecution, imprisonment, torture, and murder that they did at the hands of the Hitler-inspired authorities in Argentina and in Paraguay, Uruguay, Bolivia, and Brazil.

The consequence of this sort of variation is the likelihood that Chile might present a sustained gay culture without any noticeably dramatic confrontations with established authority, whereas the persecutions during various military regimes in Argentina during the past sixty years will have generated a contestatorial gay culture, alternately deeply underground and, during periods of redemocrati-zation, stridently countercultural. Certainly, the presence in Buenos Aires of numerous manifestations of a vital gay consciousness dur-ing the past ten years of transformation from a military into a civil society bear out such an assertion.

Brazil is yet quite a different story. That country's legendary eroti-cism—which is definitively more a question of tourism than actual fact, especially through the multinationalism of Brazilian society in recent decades, which has brought with it an increased conscious-ness of bourgeois respectability—has most traditionally been evi-dent in the carnival. The carnival is a cultural phenomenon with almost staggering homoerotic dimensions—or, at least, dimensions that go against the grain of any establishment heterosexism and Christian sexual continence (Parker; Trevisan). The neofascist mili-tary authorities that ruled in multiple variations between 1964 and the mid-1980s sought to transform the carnival as part of the over-all social transformation of a society they viewed as out of control, and this meant the commercialization of the carnival's sexuality at the necessary expense of its populist components, which included gay countercultural modalities. Sexuality may be open in Brazil, but the forces that have sought to bring transformations to Brazilian society in the name of international capitalism and participation in the multinational market (including the exploitation of that coun-try's enormously varied tourist possibilities) have contributed to a circumscription of whatever legacy of gay culture Brazil has had. This they have done in favor of a sort of polished heterosexual lib-eration, most successfully showcased by actress Sônia Braga, and most particularly in her role as the protagonist of *Dona Flor and Her Two Husbands,* the movie version of the eponymous novel by Jorge Amado (in the original Portuguese, *Dona flor e seus dois maridos;* 1966).

Amado is a writer known for his romantic socialist packaging of Brazilian populist, especially black, culture (and Amado's tra-ditional socialist background obviously means writing gay cultural out of the historical record; his vitalistic mulattos have only correct sexual tastes). This is also true of a more socially strident film such as Carlos Diegues's *Xica da Silva* (1977), in which the sexual transgressions of an eighteenth-century black slave woman, no matter how brilliantly presented as socially threatening, still leave the spectator unchallenged as regards other varieties of sexual transgression in Brazilian society.

Gay audiences may well praise a movie like *Xica* because of an important Latin American sociopolitical consideration of combining personal liberation (metonymically anchored in sexuality) with social transformation (the Latin American confirmation of the Anglo-American feminist axiom that the personal is political), but they cannot reasonably avoid meditating over why such mass-audience and often international products promote only a heterosexist image of Brazil and sustainedly avoid recording gay culture. It may be understandable why more traditional Latin American societies such as Argentina (historically, one of the leaders, along with Brazil and Mexico, in the Latin American cinematographic industry) have nothing like Spain's Pedro Almodóvar, whose films are steeped in gay sensibility, whether homosexuality is explicitly identified or not, but the absence of Brazilian gay films (alongside the steady production of the *pornochanchada*, heterosexist soft-to medium-hard pornographic films that suddenly went American in *Wild Orchid*) needs to be examined in the context of how an abiding strain of gay culture in Brazil has been circumscribed by recent major sociocultural transformations. These transformations may have contributed to producing a contained Europeanized homosexual identity whose self-image is contestatorial vis-à-vis the respectable bourgeois establishment, and even more so with the Brazilian consciousness over AIDS, at the expense of an integrated gay sensibility whose prominent manifestation throughout Brazilian social history has yet to be dealt with adequately.

Indeed, the realm of popular culture is where research must begin to reconstruct this record, because high culture in Latin America, even where it has had its social dissidents, its Bohemians with irregular tastes, historically has been in the hands of the ruling establishment, more so than in other Western societies. Latin America does have significant manifestations of a democratic, middle-class high or formal or academically respectable culture, and that culture, as in, say, the case of Nobel Prize–winning writers such as the Chilean poet Pablo Neruda and the Colombian novelist Gabriel García Márquez, put high-culture modalities (an alternative formulation might be modernist cultural practices) at the service of social transformation.

But without subtracting any merit from the goals of this production and the ways in which variations of it play a role in large-scale social consciousness, the simple fact is that high-culture print-media genres do not reach large audiences. Even in those countries where literacy reaches optimum levels, with Argentina routinely cited as the standard, economic circumstances limit considerably the individual's access to published culture. As in all of our late capitalist societies, other mass-media products fill the demand for cultural production, and only in part because they are cheaper than conventional print culture. A movie may cost a third to a fifth what a novel costs in Latin America, and although television sets are proportionately more expensive than they are in the United States or Western Europe, the fact that one set puts a large amount, if not a large variety, of programming at the disposal of extended family units makes the net cost substantially lower than most other forms of culture. Indeed, television may have provided Latin America with its most universalizing, democratizing mode of culture to date.

Yet it is not mass-media popular culture that is of interest to me here, although another critic may wish to delve into, for example, soap-opera depictions of homosexuality in a veritably enlightened fashion: say, the Venezuelan program *De mujeres* (On Women) or several Brazilian texts. But, then, this may be no more than the sort of tame incursions into so-called alternate life-styles that one can see turning up in American television programming, usually with a hidden establishment social agenda (okay, let us accept gays, but provide only images that bring them within an acceptable norm of social stability) or with the commercial exploitation of the tamely innovative, such that one cannot look to these products for anything approaching the socially transgressive or the ideologically analytical in any meaningful sense of these terms.

By the same token, it is probably not very productive to speak of a set of popular culture modalities that, in some sort of autonomous fashion, constitute a contestatorial stance toward mass-media productions, whether foreign, national, or multinational. There are those, to be sure, who would argue that folkloric culture (which in English and Spanish is also denominated as "popular," in the romantic sense of the Germanic concept of *Volk*) ought to be both prized and promoted as somehow indicative of an authentic pre-imperialistic, precapitalistic culture that constitutes the resistance of the subaltern. There is much to recommend this point of view, even when it is stripped of the high degree of sentimentalized cant in which it frequently comes enveloped as part a sectarian program, right or left. One can find in those pockets of the Latin American rural countryside still somewhat isolated from the weight of metropolitan culture and among such strata of the urban populace that still retains an identity, if only fragmentary and fading, of the millenarian cultural practices that accompanied the migration to the city manifestations of subaltern cultural identities at variance with the homogenizing, hegemonic, television-centered culture that is unifying individual Latin American countries as well as the continent. Television programming may well be the most successful multinational enterprise, just as I have previously suggested it may be the most democratic influence; however, the point is that millenarian cultural practices are disappearing under the weight of urban demographics. Latin America is more and more a society of megalopolises alongside which New York and Los Angeles are astonishingly manageable cities, and official attempts to preserve the trappings of indigenous, rural, precapitalist manifestations usually only serve to turn them into tourist attractions, which is one ungenerous way of viewing the display of autochthonous folkloric manifestations in a country like Mexico.

Rather, in this context, one wants to look for a consciously forged contestatorial culture, a cultural production that is enabled by the modernist, bourgeois concept of the artist and yet defensible as an opportunity for mass-audience resistant voices, in view of the fact that the notion of an influential, articulated subalternity cannot be possible within the parameters of dominant megalopolitan society. Certainly the contemporary novel, in its enormous range of avenues of access to a large readership on the basis of plot, world view, tone or style, character portrayal, narrative voice, and language, represents one potent intersection of high-culture production, mass-audience distribution, and opportunities for countercultural or contestatorial discourse. Consequently, it is no surprise to find that the novel has fulfilled in a "bourgeoisified" Latin American culture the same opportunities it has pursued in Europe and the United States to be an eloquent forum for the positive depiction of the gay experience and to figure narratively the ways in which that experience interacts with other social parameters while promoting its naturalization within the symbolic world shared by the novel's narrators, characters, and readers. The fact that it is no longer possible to characterize the novel in any meaningful way as either a high-culture phenomenon or a primary manifestation of popular culture—even more so with postmodernist practices of pursuing generic and modal confluences—goes a long way toward explaining why one finds narrative fiction still so important in assessing the nature and ideological fault lines of a society's cultural production.

Much more exciting, however, would be to attempt to track the manifestations of resistant culture to be found in practices that, in a global sense, are continuous with mass-media culture. I have dealt elsewhere with this possibility in the context of graphic humor and cartoon art, and there is now much interest in how such media can be used to pursue a feminist agenda. Aside from various reconsiderations of sex roles in original media productions such as the Peruvian Juan Acevedo's contra-Mickey Mouse, *Cuy* (the *cuy* is a South American rodent related to the American prairie dog), I know of no sustained gay-oriented output, although this may be more a question of honing one's reading than identifying overt relations—something like what one in a nasty mood does with Batman and Robin conjugations. Where one can begin to pick out both a gay sensibility and direct gay allusions is in popular songs. Popular music enjoys as much circulation in Latin America as it does in the United States, perhaps even more so, because radio continues to be a relatively more vital broadcast medium. But all of the channels for the distribution of popular music in the West are to be found throughout Latin American societies; cassettes, for example, are hawked in the neighborhood marketplaces alongside live chickens and medicinal herbs.

The Mexican culture critic Carlos Monsiváis, who singlehandedly has done more for the identification and legitimation of gay culture in Mexico than anyone else has for all of Latin America, has written extensively about Juan Gabriel, the son of a domestic servant whose career is a Mexican equivalent of an Elvis Presley success story. The only popular singer to perform in Mexico City's Palacio de Bellas Artes (an art deco institution that is a combined Carnegie Hall and Lincoln and Kennedy centers, one of the most prestigious high-culture institutions in Latin America), Gabriel is a cause célèbre in Mexico and adjacent Latin American countries, including the Mexican American community in the United States, because he has lived his gay identity openly. He was the one singer invited to be part of President Salinas de Gortari's official party at the July 1991 Latin American political summit in Guadalajara (and it should be noted that the singer accompanying Argentine President Carlos Menem was Susana Rinaldi, one of that country's several lesbian performers). The fact that his appeal cuts across all sorts of social lines and that the establishment openly courts him substantiates Monsiváis's implied premise that Gabriel, as a cultural icon, is a dramatic representative of a silenced component of Mexican society. And the often violent reactions to his persona (one recalls the outrage Liberace provoked in the 1950s) can be read in all sorts of Freudian ways.

Gabriel's lyrics, his delivery, and his overall cultural persona invite multiple considerations about a generalized gay sensibility for his music, something that is confirmed by the reversibility of his songs, as demonstrated in the way in which they have been reinscribed with a feminine voice by the Spanish singer Rocío Durcal. Although many of Gabriel's songs are Western saccharine love ballads in their Latin American variety, his repertory also includes compositions on overtly gay subjects, such as the one about the Noa-Noa, a famous cabaret in Ciudad Juárez frequented by gays. But what one finds particularly fascinating and susceptible to both a linguistic and a sociological analysis is the way in which many of his songs break dramatically with the love ballad's masculine-feminine dichotomy. This dichotomy is a fundamental characteristic of the love ballad. Although a male voice may quote the words of a female protagonist or a female voice may quote those of a male protagonist, the standard is either a man singing about the fortunes of his love for a woman or a woman singing about the fortunes of her love for a man. In addition to traditional sex-role behavior, reactions, and sentiments, love ballads insistently repeat generic markers so that the listener has no doubt as to who is who. The fact that Spanish is more gender marked than English only heightens this feature.

But what one finds in a significant number of Juan Gabriel's compositions is the eschewal of the conventional discourse schematics of gender. Not only are markers of the narrator and the second- or third-person object absent, but adjectives attributed to them belong to a so-called common class (or, in Latin grammar terms, the third declension) in which the form is invariable whether masculine or feminine: for example, *alegre, feliz, triste, cruel, amante, terrible,* and *mal.* These adjectives, which describe basic emotions and states, are used frequently, and much as for reasons of meter one word may be used in a song rather than its synonym, the compositions at issue here prefer the generically unmarked synonym over generically marked one: *feliz* instead of *contento/a, amante* instead of *querido/a.* It remains to be seen what a thorough analysis of Gabriel's extensive musical oeuvre can reveal in this regard, as well as to what extent this and similar practices can be identified for other singers who have attracted the attention of those responsive to gay priorities (e.g., the intensely erotic songs of another Mexican singer, Emmanuel). But it is clear that Gabriel is an important phenomenon in Latin American society regarding questions of gay cultural production.

A phenomenon like Juan Gabriel represents a present moment in Latin American popular culture. In order to add a historical dimension at this point, I would like now to turn to the Argentine tango, one of the most internationally famous Latin American cultural manifestations, especially in the renewed attention given the tango in the wake of the Paris and New York success of Pedro Segovia's *Tango argentino* in 1985 (plus traveling tour 1986–87). The tango as an almost chemically pure manifestation of masculism and macho sexual domination is notorious. But this image of the tango is based on its reputation after it became a display dance firmly anchored in lyrics that adhered to all of the traditional features of the love ballad as mentioned above, with the exception that it almost universally sings about the pathetic misfortunes of love, with a strong undercurrent of sadomasochistic violence that the dance often serves to dramatize. A close examination of the tango dance as stylized copulation (certainly the way in which all dancing by couples is routinely understood) will provide a sense of the pain-inducing dimensions of heavy, acrobatic sexual pleasure that are nowhere present in polite ballroom dancing. I have written elsewhere, however, about meanings that might be associated with the tango in its prepublic stage:

> Although the tango is pretty much an archeological
> phenomenon in Argentina, in the sense that it is associated
> with a bygone era and, like virtually all national forms of
> popular music in Latin America, it has been replaced by
> multinational products of Anglo-American inspiration, it
> has acquired a romantic aura, like the rumba and the samba,
> that is part of its international identification as characteris-
> tically Latin. The fact that it is probably associated in most
> non–Latin American minds with an image of Latin America
> as the passionate tropics says more about foreign percep-
> tions of Latin America or the ways in which Latin American
> cultural empresarios have appealed to foreign conceptions
> than it does about the sociocultural roots of the tango in the
> River Plate region. Indeed, one might want to argue that the
> Argentine tango is one thing, and American and European
> (mis)interpretations of it are quite another, although foreign
> understandings of the tango now filter back into Argentine
> perceptions. . . . (pp. 7–8)

We may identify four periods or moments in the development of the tango, depending partially on whether song, instrumental music, dance, lyrics, or combinations of them have received most attention. This complex history points to the interpenetration between the tango and Argentine social and cultural history.

The first period covers the obscure origins of the tango in the river front brothels and other "low-life" settings of Buenos Aires and Montevideo. The word itself appears to be of black African origin, related to a drum dance. There is no question that, like so many important cultural phenomena, the tango's origins are countercultural, and the problems associated with recovering all of the details of that origin are a consequence of a society's determination to ignore or destroy even oblique challenges to its conventions (and such challenges are more oblique or circumstantial than overtly disruptional). If the origin of the word tango derives from the black slaves of the River Plate shore, as a Creole cultural manifestation it is first associated with highly colloquial verses of a ribald and scatological nature that circulated among European and Middle Eastern immigrants, mestizos, mulattos, and other social outcasts on the fringes of two cities that were officially attempting to become very respectable and European. The merging of spoken verses and the dance appears to have occurred in the brothels, where risqué rhyming was a traditional pastime among waiting customers. It is reasonable to suppose that clients and employees danced together some sort of erotic step related to the complicated minuet that would become the final version of the tango. But much has been made of the fact that the tango was foremost something men danced together in these houses. No social historian has explored whether this may be taken as one of the homosexual motifs of Argentine culture that are still shrouded with almost impenetrable taboo—the male bonding of Gaucho culture and some military traditions are other potential topics of interest here. Perhaps the dance was a form of rivalry, perhaps it served to release tensions, or perhaps it served as a form of sexual arousal to be satisfied subsequently in the arms of the prostitute. Whatever one's interpretation may be, all of these factors contributed to the categoric rejection by polite society of anything associated with the tango. (Foster, "The Roots of Literary Tradition," pp. 8–9)

One need not insist on the way in which brothels are all-male worlds (and, in a projected formulation, the way in which they are microcosms of masculist society at large)[1] in which women are only shifters for the relations between men and male competition, in order to begin to associate meanings along several axes for the male-male origins of the tango as dance. To the extent that it brings together several cultural genres, that it has functioned on several social levels and serves as an index of numerous social ideologies, and that it is an icon of a global Argentine immigrant culture, the tango is a synecdoche for an entire range of cultural practices in Latin America with profound historical resonances that must be subjected to scrutiny in the recovery and analysis of homosexual components of Latin American society.

The issues that I have raised in this chapter do not propose to constitute a research agenda, at least not in the sense of a hierarchy of topics and the suggestion of appropriate methodological strategies and theoretical parameters necessary to begin to deal with them. Nor, of course, have I been able to do any more than allude to what an adequate analysis of any one of the phenomena might look like. Rather, the goal here has been to provoke interest in a range of Latin American cultural modalities that, when viewed within the appropriate sociohistorical contexts of Latin American society, ought to yield material of interest to the larger study of international gay culture. As I have suggested, such material needs to be defined along a number of lines that may not immediately suggest themselves from the perspective of research questions raised in American cultural studies, especially the need to take into account regional phenomena and the influential role played by popular culture as the potential site of significant creative innovations. Moreover, an account must be rendered of transnational circumstances, such as the culture in the United States of twenty million Latin Americans, including the different status of Mexican Americans and Puerto Rico as a Latin American enclave only partially participatory in the American cultural orbit.

Finally, although homosexuality is as much surrounded by taboo and is as much the subject of violent persecution in Latin America as it continues to be in the United States, the deeper sociocultural structures of the various Latin American societies, which include significant pre-Columbian indigenous substrata, allow for some codifications of gay sexuality radically different from what American researchers may be familiar with. Indeed, in this context, one needs to work with the premise that the similarities between the United States and Latin America in the treatment of homosexuality in some mass-media contexts may be deceptive, the result of multinational crossovers of a superficial nature. Adequate importance must be given to the way in which Latin American gay liberation, whenever it is identified as such (and it is not universally) functions more within larger sociopolitical parameters than as a question of individual rights, which has considerable implications for the forms of cultural production, the genres, and the discursive strategies the scholar is likely to focus on.

I would at this point like to extend the preceding general comments to a consideration of the writing of a specific author, the Cuban novelist Reinaldo Arenas (1943–90), and I would like to begin with a conclusion: there can be no attempt to propose a categoric definition of anything called gay sensibility, nor can any purpose be served by tracing the implications of such a sensibility for a characterization of Reinaldo Arenas's narrative. Rather, what I undertake to do, beginning with some of the thematic constellations and discourse practices to be found in Arenas—and taking into consideration major facts of his life, particularly the terrible irony of the final years of his life in New York that led him to commit suicide in December 1990—is to provide something like a prolegomenon with respect to the ideological considerations that can be raised in an approximation to the homosexual dimensions of a writer and the creative efforts of this important Cuban writer.

I would like to begin such an undertaking by recalling some of Manuel Puig's opinions in one of his final interviews in an Argentina publication to the effect that homosexuals do not exist; rather, they are the creation of a hegemonic bourgeoisie in a clinical move to circumscribe certain practices in order to render them illegitimate. It is true, to be sure, that such opinions provide a Latin American resonance to considerations that Michel Foucault has formulated throughout his writings, and, moreover, they do not go appreciably beyond what Gore Vidal proposed in the postface to the second edition of *The City and the Pillar* (1948), a pathbreaking novel of a new, postwar consciousness in the United States. Vidal asserted that there is no such thing as a homosexual in the essential sense of the verb "to be" and that there exists only homoerotic acts in which individuals whose self-conscious identity may or may not be "homosexual" participate and who may or may not participate in other bodily combinations that could be called heterosexual.

In this context, I propose the following as a first working hypothesis: a homosexual text—or, to be more precise, a text evincing a gay sensibility—would be any text that identifies itself in these terms, as in the case of the Mexican novel *Utopía gay* (1983) by José Rafael Calva. From this point of view, there can be no question of assaying a text in conceptual terms in order to determine whether or not it complies with a table of generic definitions. A text that identifies itself in these terms is entitled on its own, by virtue of the audaciousness of the act of self-identification, to become a source of knowledge of such a phenomenon. This does not mean, however, that the act of self-identification gives the text a discursive authority that cannot be questioned. What is more at issue is the matter of attaching value to the effort at textual elaboration from a specific conceptual perspective, in order to concentrate on the proposed self-denomination toward analyzing the text and confirming or repudiating what a critical reading (even when such a reading is "merely" casual) is able to attribute to it.

It goes without saying that there are few texts in our extensive

Western literary tradition overtly identified as homosexual, either directly or metaphorically. William S. Burroughs may well call one of his first novels *Queer* and Larry Kramer one of his *Faggots*. Yet there can be no question today of the homosexuality underlying works such as Oscar Wilde's *Picture of Dorian Gray,* Robert Louis Stevenson's *Dr. Jekyll and Mr. Hyde,* Walt Whitman's *Leaves of Grass,* Herman Melville's *Billy Budd,* and Henry James's *Bostonians.* In these works, explicit self-denomination yields to a "knowing" readerly frame of reference able to pick up from the texts commonplaces, allusions, and tropes confirmed explicitly in the clandestine literature of the nineteenth-century gay underworld. Such a process takes the place of the self-characterization of the texts, which would have been totally impossible within the dominant social ideology of the period (although the daring explicitness of key fragments of Whitman's poetry has led to some sleeplessness on the part of generations of U. S. literature professors, for whom the palinodes of the aging Whitman cannot help but sound quite unconvincing [Bergman 48–52; 99–100]).

The foregoing leads effortlessly to a second hypothesis: our approach to a text as belonging to the realm of gay writing is founded on those segments of the work that, in accord with a legitimate interpretive metric, can arguably be said to address issues drawn from a range of gay questions. From the perspective of this proposition, there is no demand that a text focus exclusively on a homosexual thematics, nor that the main character demonstrate the "problematic" of a gay identity. The fact is that for a certain homophobic consciousness, a homosexual text is nothing more nor less that one that turns on the "tragic curse" of perversions against nature, something seen as problematical for an individual engaged in the destruction brought about by an indecent "condition." Seen in terms of the proposals of Puig, Foucault, or Vidal, the bad faith of such a consciousness lies in the error of believing that individuals are susceptible to being portrayed exclusively in terms of a guiding and indivisible sexuality. (The same sort of consideration can be extended to an identity defined solely in terms of party affiliation, religious conviction, or ethnic and racial identity.)

The hermeneutic strategy that derives from this posture takes advantage of clusters of thematic and discursive features identifiable in the texts, which allows the critic to postulate the presence of a textual elaboration that could be called homosexual. In Arenas's case, and in a work like *Arturo, la estrella más brillante* (*Arturo, the Brightest Star;* 1984), there is no need for the text to announce itself as gay in order for the reader to grasp that the plot derives from Arturo's condition as a homosexual. The reader soon sees that the fluctuations in Arturo's existence, leading up to his suicidal attempted escape from prison and the gun blast that kills him, are the result of the improper conduct imposed on Arturo in the concentration camp where he ends up (the allusion is to Néstor Alemendro's 1984 documentary on repression in Cuba, *Conducta impropia* [Improper Conduct]).

What is involved here is a deviation assigned by the police, an imposed interpretation of a manner of being, and a system of cynical sexual exploitation in which homosexuality is confirmed by the homoerotic use to which macho jailers put the bodies of the inmates. This fact only serves to underscore the distance between a homosexual essence avoided by writers such as Arenas and Puig and the questioning of a conduct that is the result of the imposition of a hegemonic interpretation of the individual. The latter is a repressive and oppressive operation that derives as much from the bourgeois Right as it does from the Stalinist Left. What is fascinating about a text like *Arturo, la estrella más brillante,* or José Donoso's 1966 novel *El lugar sin límites* (Hell Has No Limits), is not the portrayal of "a homosexual," but the outlines of the impact on an individual of the structures of sexual power that create homosexuality as an assigned identity and not as a personally chosen series of acts. In other words, what sex acts an individual chooses to engage in is of absolutely no importance whatever, because others make violent use of his body as befits a faggot. In this way, the narrative may be seen to focus less on the identity the individual has forged for himself (a hypothesis of longstanding ingenuousness, to the extent that it overlooks the formative processes beyond his control and of which he scarcely is even conscious) in order to concentrate on the codification of certain individuals as fulfilling a role in the social dynamic assigned by force.

Of even greater interest are the references to a pattern of homo-erotic behavior in *El palacio de las blanquísimas mofetas* (The Palace of the White Skunks; 1980), to a marginalization and subsequent authoritarian violation of the body in *El mundo alucinante* (The Ill-Fated Peregrinations of Fray Servando; 1969), and to an interpersonal scheme of moral repudiation in *Vieja Rosa* (Old Rosa; 1969, a novel to which *Arturo* constitutes a sequel). In none of these cases is there a protagonist identifiable as "homosexual" on the basis of a social ideology that labels individuals so as to have a more ordered world in which even those on the fringes fulfill a function. I do not deny that homoerotic conduct is present in these novels as a set of specific acts or, perhaps, as a jouissance that juxtaposes itself to the omnipresent throes of a society undergoing an irrefutable social and moral decadence.

In *Palacio*, which could well be described as one of the most fero-cious novels of contemporary Latin American literature because of the relentless image it projects regarding the hypocrisy of so-called decency, the narrator sets himself up as implacable and all-seeing, unflinchingly scrutinizing the collapse of an synecdochal Cuban family. In this realm of dysfunction, the evolution of an awareness of the illegitimate pleasures of the flesh serves as a bulwark against the definitive breakdown of a person burdened psychologically and emotionally with a perception of the hypocrisy of the dominant con-cept of decency. At the risk of being overinsistent, it bears repeating that what is at issue is in no way the putative problems of being homosexual, but personal conduct involving a range of sexual acts of a homoerotic nature. The resonance of these acts, the manner in which they place the individual outside the law in its multiple authoritarian versions, functions to define in a denunciatory way a consciousness in the face of a hypocritical society. That society's vio-lent assault on the individual is specified by a homoerotic conduct that derives as much from the individual's assumed marginal status as from an identity imposed on him because the social dynamic re-quires, in a process of semiological differentiation, a category of sexual outlaws in order to pride itself for its decency.

A third hypothesis is that in the face of the homosexual as an entity constructed by the social dynamic, in an unimpeachable distribution of roles in the collective drama, one can speak of the forging of a homosexual identity, not in the terms of a psychological free will or voluntarism that duplicates the morality of the human being as a free agent transcending the language of the social code, but as a construct that elaborates itself within, and in opposition to, the confines of the exclusivizing definitions of the hegemonic patriarchy. To assume the degrading labels of a high-pitched morality and, in a gesture of rhetorical troping, to invest them with new meanings favorable to human dignity, is to participate in the construction of a semantic field opposed to dominant structures. The fact that this field may be essentially configured as (homo)sexual does not mean that one is backing down in the face of the categories of the dominant social interpretation: the queer in Burroughs's novel, the faggot in Kramer's novel are not individuals who passively invest themselves with the labels provided by the masters of sexual power. Rather, the terms of personal humiliation become resemanticized as bywords of a reformulated conscience of personal conduct that abruptly draws back from the domain of erotic repression. The result, if not a transcendence of the structures of sexual power (given the fact that no one can opt out of history, except through suicide), is a strategic confrontation with these structures in the name of a project for the reformulation of the social code of (homo)sexuality.

For the reader who unconsciously assimilates an antisex/homophobic hegemony or who consciously assumes its armed defense (and one here is not speaking in predominantly metaphorical terms), a writing so centered becomes a challenge to the process of interpretive decoding, to struggle against it or to assume it as a legitimate semiological configuration of social reality and the personal use of the body within it. It is in this way that the narrator of *Palacio*, in a gesture of wrenching proportions that separates him definitively from the social world in which he has been inscribed by virtue of his birth, comes to view himself, beginning with his self-identification as a witness, as a traitor to all that he contemplates:

> Está en el patio. Es de noche. Los demás duermen. La luz
> empalidece las cosas, las piedras, el fondo de las latas, sus
> manos. Y aquello llega, y aquello acosa, y lo hace superior,

fuerte, solo, terriblemente desgraciado. Está en el campo.
Es un muchacho. Desde la arboleda se oyen las voces de los
familiares que hablan en el patio mientras deshojan el maíz.
Son voces conocidas que forman la conversación corriente
de todas las tardes. Pero hay algo detrás, hay algo detrás de
aquellas palabras que sólo él comprende; y cada palabra, cada
sonido se van convirtiendo en un reto, en un terror, en una
posibilidad de ternura, en un enigma, su enigma, que solo
a él le está permitido descifrar. Pero, ¿qué se debe hacer?, a
quién debe acudir si es que alguien en este caso puede orien-
tarlo. Está en el comedor de la casa, en el pueblo. De la radio
sale una canción popular, una canción estúpida, corriente, de
esas que tanto le gustan a su prima Esther. Y también allí hay
algo que lo obliga, que lo conmina, que lo transporta, que lo
eleva, que lo deja solo con miles de interrogaciones distintas a
las que la vida cotidiana, práctica impone . . . Ahora ya es el
condenado, ya es el elegido, el que no puede conformarse; el
dueño de un espanto que no se ajusta a los estrechos límites de
las desdichas diarias. El que no puede oír una canción y decir,
oigo una canción, y es todo. El que puede oír una conversación familiar y decir, *conversan, y es todo.* El que no puede al
atardecer caminar, sencillamente por las calles, disfrutar un
instante de esa frescura, como hacen los demás, y decir, eso es
todo, sin ir más allá, sin investigar lo que no se ve, sin hacer
preguntas que, en última instancia, sólo a él le interesarían las
respuestas . . . Ahora comprendía que era justificada la des-
confianza que los otros tenían para con él. Pues, ¿qué era él
para ellos sino un traidor, alguien que se consideraba (que se
sabía) más allá, alguien que vigilaba para burlarse, alguien
que no tomaba en serio lo que para ellos justificaba la existen-
cia, sino lo *otro,* lo que nadie veía, *lo inútil?* Era un traidor.
Y, de seguir viviendo, no le quedaba otra alternativa que ser
siempre el rechazado. (160–161)[2]

Our fourth and final hypothesis underscores the way in which a society that claims to defend an antisex/homophobic norm is only able to tolerate a homosexual literature if it complies with two criteria. The first is that it be openly and unabashedly homosexual as regards theme, that it call things by their right name, which, to be sure, implies that there are stable names by which to label things, including reified human beings to be neatly filed away in the pigeonholes of the phenomenological abstractions of the hegemonic code. And second, it means giving the characters of such texts over to the executioners of that code, turning them into scapegoats whose violent end, spiritual or physical, will serve to confirm social stability, moral rectitude, and the hygiene of the bourgeois body. *Arturo* is a moving text not only because the body of the protagonist is the locus of all of the mechanisms of persecution of the individual by the blind and arbitrary power of the state, but also because Arenas records unflinchingly how one aspect of the society created by Castro duplicates the cynicism of the moral code of the very society he had sought to change through revolution.

Nevertheless, from another critical perspective, *Arturo* cannot help but reiterate the figure of the pathetic queer, the victim of his weak nature, raped by a society his neuroses prevent him from confronting forthrightly. (As, for example, is the case with the cheerful machismo of the protagonist of Guillermo Cabrera Infantes's 1979 *La Habana para un infante difunto,* a man whose open and charming erotic roguishness allows him to defy blatantly the very stultifying morality that crushes Arturo; see, however, Cabrera Infante's very sympathetic review of Arena's posthumous memoirs, *Antes que anochezca* [Before Nightfall; 1992].)

But when one turns to a novel like *El palacio de las blanquísimas mofetas,* one discovers a text whose tenor, aside from the implacable and devastatingly grotesque vision it casts regarding Cuban and Latin American society, marks it as a text that defies categorization in thematic, stylistic, and discursive terms. In addition to its condition as a paragon of a totally contingent and metonymic textuality, a delirious fugue through time and space and the mentalities of its characters (in line with the image on the cover of the first Venezuelan edition of Death careening out of control on a bicycle), *Palacio* proposes the total disarticulation of the structures of bourgeois knowledge regarding the world described, which, in more than one formulation, constitutes the crux of gay sensibility. Because the gay can never be a question of a close psychosexual classification that freezes the individual in his position within the network of the dominant social code, it must then become a way of viewing social organization in terms of a radical contingency that once and for all breaks out of the prison house of historical language: "Pero si algo permanecía fijo en él era la condición fatal, inexplicable—entonces—de encargado de administrar los gritos" (159).[3]

Once the question can be seen in this way, much more than *Arturo* (a novel that I have examined at length elsewhere; *Gay and Lesbian Themes* 66–72), *Palacios* could well turn out to be the text most characterized by the gay sensibility of a writer who took his life as the final consequence of assuming with great honesty the role of being the one who did the shouting: "Viejos desgraciados, lo que nunca les perdonaré no es que me hayan traído a este mundo, sino que me hayan obligado a quedarme en él" (39).[4]

I have, up to this point, discussed gay writing as it relates to a male production, and it is now time to speak of a lesbian work. An initial difficulty is the simple fact that if one wishes to avoid the clinical term *homosexuality,* proper to medical and criminal discourses, only in certain tentatively conventional uses does the term *gay* cover both men and women; indeed, lesbian identity customarily marks itself off as distinct from gay identity (see, e.g., Fuss's *In/side Out: Lesbian Theories, Gay Theories*). The only convenient umbrella term is the adjective of the emergent denomination Queer Theory (as in the special issue of *différances*), but *queer* has rather problematical resonances unless it is definitively understood as re-semanticized. Because it is now widely acknowledged that lesbian and gay are not simply converses of each other, because of the radically different history of women's experience in our society (Faderman), one cannot merely take on lesbian writing as an adjunct to that of the gay. Yet this is of course what I am doing here, but less as a disingenuous example of tokenism than to balance the discussion of one male text, Arenas's novel, with comments on a female novel,

Sara Levi Calderón's *Dos mujeres*, (*The Two Mujeres;* 1990)—because I wish to make a case for how the question of lesbian/gay/ queer sensibility involves the same set of premises espoused in the opening sections of this chapter.

The first overt Latin American novel on a male homosexual theme was published in Brazil in 1895 (Adolfo Caminha's *Bom Crioulo*); the first Mexican one in 1964 (Manuel Barbachano Ponce's *El diario de José Toledo* [The Diary of José Toledo]). The first Latin American novel to contain significant lesbian material is also from Brazil: Aluísio Azevedo's *O cortiço* (The Tenement; 1890). The first Mexican lesbian novel is Rosamaría Roffiel's *Amora* (1989). The are several ways of explaining this interesting gap of one century, and undoubtedly one would begin with the significant differences in the sociocultural histories of the two countries and the relatively different roles afforded women of all classes with regard to subject positioning and sexual identity. In the case of Mexico, a social history of literature (and of culture in general) would out of necessity have to make reference to something like a social pact that, for many centuries, severely restricted the range of what could be published in Spanish. Indeed, one could make a case of how the efficaciousness of that social pact imposed limits on what Mexican authors *wished* to write about as much as on what they *were permitted* to write about. Unquestionably, this has much to do with the various forms of censorship imposed in the New World by the Spanish Empire and the Inquisition and with the complex factors effecting Mexican nation formation after both early nineteenth-century independence and after the 1910 revolution.

The impression one has—and I stress that it is only an impression, not borne out by requisite empirical research—is that foreign literature has constituted something like a privileged space. Until recent explosive changes in Mexico within the context of the multinationalization of, at least, urban Mexican society. This would also include the imposition of what Fredric Jameson has called the cultural logic of late capitalism. By this I mean that, until these changes, readers have reserved for the sphere of foreign literature, whether in the original or in Spanish translation, a spectrum of human experiences that has included most of the daily realities of sexuality. To be sure, there is a tradition of writing about female prostitution, centering on Federico Gamboa's *Santa* (1903), and there is a lush garden of fleshly dimensions yet to be taxonimized sufficiently in Amado Nervo's poetry. But there have been strident reactions to recent works such as Luis Zapata's *Las aventuras, desventuras y sueños de Adonis García, el vampiro de la Colonia Roma* (Adonias García; a Picaresque Novel; 1979) on, among other sexually dissident subjects, sexual cruising and male prostitution; Angeles Mastretta's *Arráncame la vida* (Mexico Bolero; 1986), which is admirably frank and, therefore, profoundly disturbing for those still committed to the myths of feminine modesty; and, of course, Roffiel's *Amora* and Levi Calderón's *Dos mujeres,* the other Mexican novel to rend the curtain of concealment in Mexico regarding lesbian love. (I think it is significant to note here that Roffiel's novel was issued by Planeta Mexicana, part of an international publishing conglomerate.)

Of course, one could argue that despite all the caveats, there has been a long and distinguished tradition of gay poetry in Mexico, especially associated with the Contemporáneos group in the 1920s and 1930s. Carlos Monsiváis has done much to bring this production to our attention (e.g., Monsiváis, *Amor perdido* 265–96). But the fact that the personal memoir of Salvador Novo, on whom Monsiváis focuses, has only been published in English (Leylan *Now the Volcano* 11–51) and that only scattered allusions exist to the homoeroticism of Xavier Villaurrutia and Jaime Torres Bodet, among others, only serves to confirm the silence.

To be sure, numerous foreign novels dealing with ripe sexuality—paradigmatically, American best sellers—have circulated openly in Mexico. But it wasn't that long ago that Editorial Diana (the publisher of Levi Calderón's novels) ran into trouble from the guardians of morality with John Rechy's *City of Night* (1963; a novel that foreshadows Zapata's *Adonis García* by almost twenty years), which is one of the reasons this important Chicano author has been issued in countless languages and yet has been loathe to authorize any further Spanish translations. But then, of course, there is a profound difference between the superficial sexual hydraulics of best selling narratives and the far-ranging challenges to the hegemony of the monogamous, anerotic, and heterosexist patriarchy of the novels signed by Rechy, Zapata, Mastretta, and Roffiel. And there is also a profound difference between texts that address themselves to the structures of the patriarchy as they function in an alien setting and challenges to those structures that are evinced at home by one's own father, brother, husband, or lover. Finally, there is yet another profound difference between eroticism, whatever its bodily conjugations, as it is expressed in poetry (and here we can speak of roots extending as far back as sor Juana Inés de la Cruz, as Octavio Paz, to his evident chagrin, was forced to do) and in the far more public forum of the novel or theater (cf. the problems Jesusa Rodríguez has experienced; on Sor Juana's lesbian primacy, see Bautista).

I have written elsewhere (*Gay and Lesbian Themes* 114–18) about Roffiel's *Amora,* and I conclude my comments on that novel with the following key passage that illustrates the transgressive *écriture feminine* of lesbian writing:

> Nos imagino tomando té, las dos muy juntas, contándonos cómo, a veces, la menstruación nos abre más los sentidos y nos conduce de los ovarios a la creación. O, al contrario, nos aleja de ella. Cómo, con la sangre, mujeres nuevas se posesionan de nosotras, algunas conmovedoramente cercanas; otras, ajenas y terribles. Porque nuestra sangre mensual encierra la ferocidad y el color de la vida, pero también el germen de la locura. (148)[5]

Levi Calderón's *Dos mujeres,* only the first in what one hopes will be a long line of books to follow the lead of Roffiel's work, was first issued in April 1990, and it was reprinted in September of that year. An English translation, prepared by Gina Kaufer in consultation with the author (which legitimates the changed ending of the text) was issued in San Francisco by Aunt Lute Books in 1991 with the title of *The Two Mujeres*—preserving the word *mujeres* (women) rather than translating it, thereby suggesting for it a privileged semantic scope. *Dos mujeres* is the story of a sentimental and erotic relationship between two artists, Genovesa, a painter, and Valeria, the narrator-novelist; Levi Calderón's novel is coextensive with the one Valeria is writing concerning her relationship with Genovesa. Eschewing the tragic mode of classical male gay writing (e.g., Caminha's aforementioned *Bom Crioulo* or Luis Zapata's *En jirones* [1985]), but also the often facile and yet so necessary utopian celebratory mode of the dominant strain of American lesbian writing (cf. the bulk of works issued by Naiad Press), Levi Calderón opts for what one might call a relentlessly sociological mode. On the one hand, her love story examines microscopically all of the tensions and turmoils, euphorias and setbacks of any amatory relationship, with its complex protocols of intimate interpersonal relations. But the refusal to cast the complexities of an erotic relationship in a tragic mode, even when it becomes specifically identified as lesbian, is the ideologically significant rejection of the tiresome hypothesis that homosexual love is any more star-crossed than sentimental unions in general. On the other hand, Levi Calderón is unflinching in the portrayal of the obstacles two women in love must overcome in an aggressively phallocentric society.

Valeria comes from an upper-middle class family of Lithuanian immigrants who arrived in Mexico before World War II. Her father makes his fortune in construction and, in typical capitalist fashion (he is reminiscent of Fuentes's Artemio Cruz), diversifies his holdings, turning everything he touches into money. Circumscribed by the bourgeois conventions of her family's social aspirations and by the religious conventions of their immigrant Judaism, which is more cultural than religious, Valeria can only stake out her emotional, sexual, and artistic freedom through enormous determination and multiple physical torments. Her father attempts to batter her into submission; her brother considers himself an extension of the wrathful hand of Jehovah; she marries an abusive husband; and her sons persecute her mercilessly when she fails to comply with the Virgin-of-Guadalupe maternal role expected of every Mexican woman, irrespective of her social condition.

Levi Calderón does not handle the physical abuse to which Valeria is subject as a metaphor for the patriarchal prison from which the woman must free herself in order to pursue honestly her erotic needs. Rather, it is quite literally consonant with documented strategies for imposing social and sexual conformity in one Latin American society, which perhaps explains, in another dimension, why gay male writing in Mexico has been so assertive, whereas lesbian writing has until now been so absent: the one has sought to affirm itself with a considerable ingenuity of formats, being at the same time an extension of phallocentric privilege; the other has had almost incalculable circumscriptions to overcome. (All of this is said on the assumption that lesbian culture in Mexico, which has most assuredly always existed, has had to express itself in nonpublic ways—that is, in other than the privileged genres of prestige culture—that have yet to be documented. This is especially so if one subscribes to Adrienne Rich's hypotheses concerning the lesbian continuum.)

One could be troubled by the fact that Levi Calderón's women are drawn from privileged social classes, while recalling that in a sense such classes are ironically more controlled in their private lives than individuals on the overlooked margins. Valeria is undoubtedly able to make skillful use of her advanced education and her talent as a writer to record and to interpret the passage from hegemonic patriarchy to the fluidity of lesbian erotics, but it is precisely her social privilege that leaves her more exposed to the processes of social technology. The demands of class, the conformist urgencies of immigrant subcultures, and the overcompensation of especially marginalized subcultures such as the Jews in Latin America, often so concerned not to do anything that would lend credence to anti-Semitic stereotypes—one must not give *shande far di goyim* (shame in front of non-Jews)—such multiple enmeshings can almost make living on the socioeconomic margins look utopian.

Needless to say, the fact that Valeria is a Jew is a far from subtle play on questions of fascistic authoritarianism and the persecutions of the detested Other: the victims of persecution become themselves the victimizers of the despised alien, their lesbian daughter, thereby violating the daughter's obligation to subject herself to the father. (Given the Jewish dimension of the novel, Theweleit's research on Nazi male sexual fantasies is particularly pertinent here.) And, too, the central part of the novel recounts Valeria's life before Genovesa, with an emphasis on personality development that does little to promote a questioning of classical psychoanalysis. Yet this segment reads enough like the script of an outrageous soap opera to insinuate the beginnings of a questioning of Lacanian motifs of the phallic order.

Much has been made in feminist theory, and even more so in its application to lesbianism, of the need to not just write women's experience but to question the master codes by which that experience is written:

> [The] paradox of history and origins in lesbian novels is related to and perhaps creates and sustains a similar paradoxical structure of desire that typifies lesbian accounts. While the drive of conventional history is to know, lesbian fictional histories frustrate the possibility of total knowledge and define the desire for mastery as unfulfillable from the start. Not fulfilling the desire to know sustains desire, continues it so that desire, like history, is a paradox: to desire is to desire not to have a desire fulfilled; it is the desire for an unfilfilled desire. (Roof 111; Zimmerman, passim; cf. Pérez on Chicana lesbians and Franco on Mexican feminist literary structure in general)

Experience does not exist free of such master codes, and, indeed, those codes serve in great measure to define what is understood as experience and to mold interpretations of it. I am, of course, speaking here under the purview of Foucault's propositions concerning discursive formations. A corollary of these hypotheses has been to argue that the very notion of plot, at least in the Proppian sense of a morphology of the narrative, of a coherent narratology, is phallocentric, and that one of the contributions of feminist discourse must legitimately be not just a revision of the master plots, not just their accommodation to the "plots" of women's experience, but even the possibility of transcending the notion of plot as somehow intrinsically authoritarian by virtue of the expectations that plots impose on our negotiations of human experience. Thus a contestatorial feminist work such as Levi Calderón's can properly write against the grain of plot expectations, even if it does not in the end suspend them. This is immediately evident in the rejection of the paradigmatic plot of homosexual pathos—from a lesbian perspective, Hall's classic *Well of Loneliness* (1928) or, in American literature, Patricia Highbridge's pseudonymously published *Price of Salt* (1952). But it is also evident in passages like the following, which, although it may not be privative of feminist discourse, illustrates well the sort of associative writing that permits the suspension of plot logic or imposes significant variations on it:

UNA DANZA VIOLETA . . .
Imágenes de agua y viento. Los tres, sentados en un sofá verde raído, miran hacia el frente. Janosh, con su nariz insoportablemente chueca, se endereza. Moran, sentada sobre el brazo del sofá, se detiene de él. Genovesa se dirige al tocadiscos para ponerle más volumen. Patti Smith canta *Horses*. Genovesa en cuclillas, sigue el ritmo. Su falda oscura de flores amarillas ondea en sentido contrario a sus caderas. Johny saca una filosa navaja; de un tajo se corta la yugular; cae lentamente sobre las arenas mojadas de la playa; un tropel de caballos viene hacia él; de sus hocicos aterciopelados brotan llamas de un rojo profundo. *There's a little place called space / The waves were comin in like radiant stallions / There's a little place called space / A promised land*. Genovesa, con los brazos extendidos, se impulsa hacia arriba, vuelve a ocupar su lugar junto a Janosh.
   El hilo de esta historia es acompañado por el seco golpeteo de unos cepillos metálicos. Los tres personajes frente a mí parecen la fotografía de un rock asesino. El tiempo transcurre sin que las tinieblas fulfurantes de mi mente se aclaren. (194)[6]

Now, one could argue that this sort of writing is not substantively different from earlier "surrealist" modes or the free-association writing of novels from the countercultural sixties. And up to a point, that is true. However, it must be remembered that I initially characterized Levi Calderón's novel as being written within an essentially sociological mode, and I am hard put to identify documentary or testimonial texts by male authors that are so willing as *Dos mujeres* to mix modes in the fashion implied by a juxtaposition of sociological exposition and hallucinous free association (or, to use an alternate term, *delirious eroticism*). In any case, the question as to whether there is, from the point of view of style or discourse a specifically feminine *écriture* has been vigorously debated, and recent thinking has tended to put the emphasis on the way in which a feminist discourse arises not from any intrinsically "womanly aesthetics" deriving from women's bodies and their specific experiences, but with concrete ideological formations that call forth concomitant discursive practices, such as the sort of conjunction of the sociological and the hallucinatory I have recorded for Levi Calderón's novel (Felski; Suleiman).

Valeria and Genovesa do, in the end (*pace* the use of a plot concept), achieve a satisfactory union, but only in a Paris far removed from the oppressive structures of their Mexican passage. The return to Europe for Valeria is not without its resonances (the same could be said of Levi Calderón's current residence in San Francisco), for the freedom from persecution her parents sought in one corner of the New World proved, at least for their daughter, the bitterest deception of all. Perhaps it has been this aspect of Levi Calderón's novel, the attainment of a satisfactory union and the relinquishment of the subject position of the legendary Mexican (and Jewish) matriarch, more than any scandalous erotics, that most sparked outrage when it was published, that most underwrote it as a transgressive reinscription, to use Dollimore's useful concept, of the social pact. All of which, of course, make it an immediate Mexican best seller.

> O saldo mais positivo disso tudo foi justamente a evidência de que o pé representa pra muita gente algo ao mesmo tempo muito erótico e muito desconhecido. Conseqüentemente, posso dizer que tive enorme êxito, na medida em que despertei essa sensibilidade naqueles poucos que me procuraram e coloquei a minhoca na cabeça dos muitos outros que leram a circular mas não tiveram vontade ou coragem de me contatar. Mesmo que a maioria destes não transe homem, provavelmente terão curiosidade de provar o erotismo pedal

com a própria esposa ou namorada. Isso é importantíssimo, pois quanto mais gente se interessar por pés e mais a mística se difundir, melhor pra mim, já que por tabela aumentam minhas chances de encontrar alguém com cabeça feita. (Mattoso, *Manual de pedólatra amador* 153)[7]

If Foucault is correct concerning the history of sexuality, the insistence with which Western culture has created a discourse about sex—has, indeed, created a concept of sexuality, since the seventeenth century—has tended not to repress a healthy or natural sexual instinct but to provide that instinct with a technology that will enable it to be channeled in ways suitable to the sociopolitical economy of the modern world. Thus those who would believe that sexual liberation, whether hetero- or homosexual, involves the cancellation of a discourse of repression would seem to be missing the point: some forms of sexual activity *are* repressed, but others are encouraged, and in either case it is a question of providing sexual activity with an ideology that inscribes it in a macrodiscourse of social acts, including both the public and the private. Any goal of sexual liberation must by definition, therefore, mean a reideologization of sexuality and a redefinition of social macrodiscourses, and not simply the renegotiation of putatively private acts with no regard for their transindividual social contexts.

Indeed, the contemporary proliferation of sexual treatises and manuals about the conduct of sex, aside from being part of the generalized industry of mass-media popular knowledge about everything, underscores the technological dimension of sex for modern individuals: what we know serves to substantiate social macrodiscourses, and social macrodiscourses serve to establish the parameters of what we need to, ought to, or even can know. Even a work like *The Joys of Gay Sex*, decidedly written with a liberational ideology, is circumscribed not by the limits of the body (or by a body viewed as unbounded by convention and prejudice) but by what we can at the moment understand the body and its boundaries to be, a principle that may perhaps help us to understand the debate over the erotic legitimacy of sadomasochism.

It flows from the foregoing, if not inevitably, certainly at least not unexpectedly, that the technology of sexuality will go hand-in-hand with the technologization of modern life in general, and that the fonts of an overall technological knowledge will also be the sources of our technology of sex: the focal points of hegemonic technology will also be the producers of a contemporary sexual code, and the most cursory bibliographic review will, in fact, reveal that American bourgeois sexual education, often in its most liberal variety, is the model, whether through translation or imitation, of the technology of sex in hegemonized societies. This, of course, does not mean that alternative sexual discourses do not exist. Indeed, one aspect of sexual tourism for the (at least male) citizen of the hegemonic culture (Havana holidays for Eisenhower Americans; R&R in Tokyo for the Vietnam conscript; carnival in Rio for readers of the *Advocate*) is the opportunity to step outside the prevailing sexual discourse, even if it only means that other sexual discourses may themselves be part of a technology of sex and maybe even one that, for all its appearances as another way of erotic life, is in reality generated in some perverse and cynical way by the hegemonic one.

Ripe brothel sex in pre-Castro Havana, including all of the wonders of gay life, ought certainly to be viewed as an integral part of post–World War II sexual ideology in the United States. But such considerations aside, to the extent that some common denominator of Western late-capitalist hegemony has not yet penetrated to every corner of the world and that, in fact, there are significant so-called Third World social constellations *within* the United States, one universal technology of sex is still more of an ideal than reality. Thus for those who choose to believe that universalization of culture will never be a completed project (postmodernism does have its theoretical blessings, after all), their scanning of sexual metadiscourses for signs of fissure or rupture will not necessarily be an exercise in futility.

The question, then, would become not whether hegemonic technology in matters of sexuality will reign supreme, but where should one look for the counterdiscourses. Even before the question is asked, there is a ready answer in the realm of cultural production, as either the return of the repressed despite the best efforts on the part

of the reproducers of the dominant code or, clearly more significantly, as part of the concerted effort to exploit ideological incongru-
encies in the hegemonic code on the part of contestatorial writers.
A quick survey of commercial versus noncommercial cultural production in America will provide abundant examples for each, with
perhaps a commercial phenomenon such as rock and roll being the
most magnificent return of the repressed in our society (one betrays
one's age by still being able to recall the injunctions against the sin-
fulness of the young Elvis in the 1950s), and gender-conscious writing in recent years representing a concerted block of repudiators of
the dominant code in multiple dimensions. Concomitantly, the cultural production of subaltern or nondominant societies constitutes
the most fertile ground for confronting transnational technological dominance, and there is now the firmly entrenched perception
that postmodernism in a sector of the world such as Latin America
must be understood less as the extension of First World domination and more as a cluster of strategic positions against globalizing
technologies of control and assimilation.

Leaving aside the long list of foreign (mostly, U.S.) best sellers in
Spanish and English translation, Latin American bookstores are divided between an inventory of nativist production in culture (understood here in the narrow sense of traditional genres and their close
mutations) and an inventory of nonnativist publications (mostly in
translation) of the technologies of the dominant, transnational social
discourse. By the same token that one is not likely to find manuals for computer programs (or, computer programs to begin with)
in anything other than translation from English, one is equally un-
likely to find treatises on sexuality in anything other than translation: Masters and Johnson; the *Joys* series; even, I would venture,
Dr. Ruth.

It is certainly not that the member of a nonhegemonic society (or
a member of a hegemonized society who establishes a self-identity
as yet nonhegemonic) cannot write a sexual treatise other than one
that is demonstrably derivative of hegemonic models (like the many
Brazilian scientific treatises about sex Parker discusses under the
heading of the production of a scientific analysis of sex in Brazil
in the late nineteenth and early twentieth centuries). Rather, the

question becomes the extent to which there is likely to be a market for indigenous technologies of sex, any more than there is likely to be a market for indigenous technologies of any other sort. Surely a market does exist for radically divergent technologies, those that set themselves up as diametrically opposed to the dominant ones, in which there is a subtext of categorical opposition to the process of hegemonization. I have in mind here best-selling treatises on the occult in Argentina or on spiritism in Brazil: in both cases hegemonic science as much as institutionalized religion is undermined by these alternative discourses, which most assuredly would contain alternate versions of sexuality, if only by implication.

But the dominant discourse challenges these discourses as nonscientific, and although such a challenge is probably not very successful, to judge by reports about sales, it does propose a dramatic parting of the waters that assumes radically different readerships. But what I am speaking of is the possibility of a technological discourse that as alternative or contestatorial as it may be, is yet firmly inscribed, if only nominally, within the conventions of scientific language. Such efforts undoubtedly exist, but my premise here is that it can only be a foregone conclusion that they are doomed to insignificance, not by their intrinsic quality but by the conditions of knowledge acquisition within which they must compete.

If, then, there is to be in a sector of the world like Latin America an alternative technology of sexuality, other than cultural production in the narrow sense of the term, it must assume radically different dimensions than either those of science-as-usual or those of a confrontational repudiation of science. What I would like to explore here is one such effort, Glauco Mattoso's *Manual do pedólatra amador; aventuras & leituras de um tarado por pés* (Manuel of the Amateur Foot Lover; Adventures and Readings of Someone Wild about Feet; 1986), the first volume in a series entitled *Boca do inferno* and supplemented by a comic-book version, with illustrations by Marcatti, *As aventuras de Glaucomix o pedólatra* (The Adventures of Glaucomix the Foot Lover; 1990). To begin with, one might well argue that Mattoso's "treatise" is merely a notable example of marginal narrative, a postmodern novel passing as the author's first-person erotic biography passing, in turn, as a sex manual. Such a characterization of *Manual* is a legitimate one, and, were libraries to own it (it seems only to exist in the United States in the Library of Congress), it might as well be classified under Brazilian fiction (PQ) as under sexual treatises (HQ), or perhaps even under facetiae (PN). But what I would like to do here is to examine the ideological implications of reading Mattoso's *Manual* as a valid, albeit especially outrageous, entry in a bibliography of alternate technologies of sex.

Let us begin with an initial characterization of *Manual* as outrageous. Having proposed such a qualifier, I hasten to add that I mean it in no way to be taken as pejorative. Indeed, in the context of a postmodernist aesthetic, any deviation—sexual or rhetorical or the two combined—that may be judged to be outrageous can, in fact, constitute considerable praise. Rather than insinuate a dismissive attitude toward the text because of its failure to abide by the conventions of common-ground discourse—an adherence to a balanced objectivity having the goal of not alienating the timorous reader—the outrageous text establishes in an aggressive manner its credentials as a transgressive voice whose "authority" (the scare quotes serve here to remind us of the oxymoronic nature of a conjugation of the sort "transgressive authority") the reader is willing to accept for the moment. For the purposes of the argument, toward seeing where it might lead, reasonably or otherwise, the reader sees the authority not as inherent (as in the case of established authority) but as an apophantic.

Mattoso's text is outrageous along several axes. In the first place, it is frankly autobiographic, with nary an apology for its scandalous nature or the fact that the sexual deviations it describes are recounted without any trace of mediating rhetoric of moral exculpation ("this is gruesome stuff, but it is, regrettably, human nature as it really is"). Mattoso's account of a sexual education, autobiographical or otherwise, is not framed by the naturalistic conventions of pseudoscientific writing, which serves to posit a vivid dividing line between the moral superiority of the pact shared by reader and narrator (who has transcended the moral abyss of what is narrated) and a stoutly contemplated human corruption. Rather, the suspension of moral distancing accomplished by an unrepentant first-person narrator and the unmediated (at least by implied or explicit authoritarian judgments) chronicle of the sexual facts of life is what provides the basically outrageous coloration of Mattoso's joyful personal memoir.

That this memoir is that of a foot fetishist, and not an abstract fetishist, but one grounded, so to speak, in the grit and grime of the individual's fundamental physical contact with the dirt of the earth, is yet another dimension of the *Manual*'s outrageous texture. Mattoso might well have in some metaphorical fashion poeticized his fetish. But by anchoring his discourse in the colloquial Brazilian word *chulé* (something like an omnibus word centered on the English trope "toe jam"), Mattoso means for his reader never to lose sight of the fact that he is dealing, literally, with the slime of history. Indeed, the repudiation of the civilized practice of foot-washing and supplementary fragrances, along with an underscoring of the foot as it comes enclosed in its most proletarian guises, maintains a materiality for the narrator's fetish that effectively blocks any desire of the reader to slip into allegory or any sort of metonymic process that will detour the discourse into means other than the primally literal: multiple attentions devoted to the unadorned foot as an erotic locus in its own right. It is one thing to subscribe to the cheerful notion that the entire body, in every single one of its folds and protuberances, is a unified erogenous zone, and it is quite something else to accord egalitarian attention to each one of those details in an unprejudiced sexual practice that frees one from hypostatized territories and attendant regulating hygienes.

Finally, Mattoso's conjugation of pediphilia and homosexuality is outrageous. To be sure, the regulating notion of homosexuality holds it as inherently outrageous, while hypostatizing such a corporeal intercourse in terms of a presumed dominant anality; such a territorial prejudice, of course, merely accommodates homosexuality within a preexisting, reductionary hypostasis of heterosexual acts as a commerce of the penetrating and the penetrated. By first inscribing his fetish within a homosexual matrix and then defying presumed anal-dominant conventions of homosexuality by relocating primary erogeny to the foot, Mattoso's narrator adds exponential increments to the outrageous quality of his text. Such strategies are accompanied by derivations of the decision to locate the text in the lexical realm of the *chulé*—that is, by an unrelenting stylistic commitment to a colloquial register of Brazilian Portuguese that, if it only makes reading arduous for the nonnative speaker, renders the *Manual* quite offensive for all but the most indulgent of native speakers. Indeed, native speakers, because they appreciate the nuances of the language, have greater reason for separating themselves from the text than do nonnative speakers, who may simply find it at times incomprehensible.

Let us analyze for a moment Mattoso's first-person narrative. Certainly, the function of such an ostensibly "direct" voice cannot serve merely to legitimize the text, as the content of the adventures described therein are sufficiently deviant from the social norm as to render superfluous any appeal to narrator/reader identity. Yet in a converse and perverse way, the first-person narrator of the *Manual* does, in fact, encourage an identity between narrator and narratee in a dimension the latter may not have hitherto dared to contemplate: Mattoso speaks in his own voice—again, deftly juggling variations and dimensions of an outrageous discourse—in order to establish and confirm an allegiance between that voice and those individuals who may not previously have had at their disposal a sexual discourse suitable to their needs, suspected or otherwise.

This leads me to what I consider to be the most salient point to be made about Mattoso's textual practice, one that is confirmed in the alternation between first-person confessions, quotations from literary and paraliterary sources (approximately 160 pages of text are complemented by 98 footnotes), and sundry pseudorealia (letters from friends, responses to personal ads, and the transcript of a closing dialogue with Sylvia). The point is the way in which a discourse like that of the *Manual,* by contrast to (pseudo)scientific writing and literary fabulation, involves processes designed to provoke the liberalization or the carnivalization of sexual signifiers. That is to say, the *Manual* represents a radical break with a "sensible" analysis of sexuality (with all of the legislative meanings attached to this term) in order to range over various dimensions of the sexual experience toward, essentially, placing every form of behavior under analytical scrutiny. If normative homosexuality is defied when the narrator experiences his only "heterosexual" act with a woman who latter turns out to be a lesbian, a woman with whom he subsequently establishes a stable interpersonal relationship, the very coming together of Mattoso and Sylvia, first as a "straight" couple and then as two individuals each with an assumed homosexual identity, does little to reconfirm the social primacy of heterosexual marriage. And if pediphilia has as its most eloquent endorsement the possibility of "continuar transando numa boa sem risco de AIDS" (back cover), it can only function as a powerful turn-on for the narrator in its most strident dimension of *sexo sujo* (dirty sex). By recontextualizing sexual experience in terms of an erogenous zone that defies all of the Western culturemes of cleanliness, the *Manual* jejunely defies its readers to exceed limits that they might not even have imagined to exist. All of these textual strategies are moves in a process of turning sexual signifiers into a free-floating process of meanings that have little to do with standard sex manuals, whether hetero- or homosexual (cf. 35–36, 68–69).

This sort of analytical assessment of options, founded on an appeal to concrete personal experience, with the latter being reinforced by a colloquial register complemented by circumstantial word plays, is what distances Mattoso's exposition from a First World sexual treatise, anchoring it the specific sociocultural context of the Rio de Janeiro and São Paulo sexual underworld of the 1970s and early 1980s (underworld not just because it is marginal sexuality, but because Brazil was still under dictatorship, a fact to which Mattoso makes reference when he speaks of the censorship of "immoral" gay publications with which he was associated). This appeal to a grounding in personal experience is especially evident when the narrator interfaces details of his desires and erotic undertakings with the written record, frequently drawn from American sources (and quoted in the original English):

> Como o leitor terá notado, tais contos nada mais eram que uma transposição de minhas experiências reais *para um plano ligeiramente mais fantástico*. Coisa que agora até se afigura supérflua, em face deste livro onde estou relatando tudo em suas proporções exatas. (120; emphasis added)[8]

It should be noted here that the above statement refers to one of Mattoso's own texts, which he quotes in the original Portuguese and then in the English translation in which it circulated internationally in the Leyland anthology.

On another occasion, the narrator complains of the annoying reticence of texts in the reporting of the actual facts of physical suffering, a suffering that for him constitutes a crucial erotic dimension:

> De fato, o que há muito me irritava era a enxurrada de livros de "memórias" de vítimas da repressão, que pretendiam denunciar as violências sofridas, mas que, por pudores moralistas ou escrúpulos ideológicos, se auto-censuravam justamente no momento de descrever as cenas de tortura, sobretudo os lances sexuais implícitos ou explícitos, os quais acabavam sistematicamente omitidos ou eufemizados. (123)[9]

Indeed, the dimension of Mattoso's personal record that underscores his interest in sadomasochism points to one of the most ideologically problematic aspects of his texts—that is, an instance in which it becomes most specifically outrageous in the context of objective sexual treatises. It is not just that Mattoso defends sadomasochism's legitimate appeal as an erotic impulse. This is a position that has produced serious rifts in gay writing, and one can compare the negative images provided, from a male point of view, in John Rechy's novel *Rushes* with the positive ones, from a female point of view, in Pat Califia's stories in *Macho Sluts*. Califia's collection contains an important essay in defense of lesbian sadomasochism: sadomasochism is frequently viewed as problematical because it, among other things, ritualizes the homosexual's position as victim and outcast, with lesbian sadomasochism adding the dimension of women's generalized experience as the object of sexual violence (see Dworkin). Yet Mattoso makes it clear that he is defending sadomasochism, not from a "Nazi" perspective of the appropriate domination of the weak by the strong, but as a form of sexual theatrics where rituals of symbolic humiliation, not actual physical torment, are at issue (145; this is also the sense of the quote, "Sim, porque tortura de verdade, na própria pele, nem morta!" [36]).[10]

Mattoso's distinction between actual torture and sadomasochism as a form of sexual theatrics (although he does recognize, as many commentators on official torture have, that the former inevitably involves a dimension of the latter, at least for the torturer; see Liliana Cavani's 1974 film *The Night Porter*) does not, however, exhaust this one highly problematic dimension of his outrageous defense of pediphilia. Mattoso proceeds to defend not so much the erotic resonances of actual political torture as the use of such accounts as ingredients in his own erotic psychodrama, in which the descriptions of the torments inflicted on others in the name of a political economy can properly be recoded to serve as stimuli in an arena of personal sexual pleasure. Rather than questioning the validity of such a transcoding and eschewing a consideration of how politically correct readers might find such an operation cynical, to the extent that it becomes complicitous with the legitimation of political torture, Mattoso's autobiographical narrator segues into a consideration of such texts as erotically inadequate because they stop short of providing the sort of explicit details about eroticized suffering his personal interests require. Rather than addressing the question as to why such silences and euphemisms are present in the texts of the memoirs of survival—a discursive analysis of such writing (which Mattoso has no obligation to engage in) might begin with what can and what cannot be spoken, given the inaugural abyss between the knowledge of the narrator and the "outsiderness" of the narratee—the narrator as writer contemplates the need, which is, after all, the starting point of the *Manual,* to create his own erotic discourse (124).

Just as Mattoso concerns himself with defending his pediphilic interpretation of literary texts that foreground the foot, he equally eschews theorizing his desire to read erotically the memoirs of the survivors of political torture, failing even to recognize the substantive, real-life differences between the two categories of discourse. The indiscriminate conjugation of the two constitutes one of the most outrageous, if not ideologically troublesome, aspects of the

Manual. But the fact is that Mattoso dispenses with both forms of writing as inadequate to his own expressive needs, and it is in the space cleared by the furlough given both literature and prison memoirs that the *Manual* is able to emerge, grounded in a highlighted personal experience that validates itself, *not* by the confirmation of images in other sources but by its putative singularity. Indeed, Mattoso's principal autoconfirmation will come from the reader response he records to earlier versions of experiences, all sustained by varieties of the same topos.

The transgressive panerotics of sexual desire that Mattoso's narrative puts in motion on the basis of the multiple dimensions of outrageousness I have described, ranging from the narrator's basic erotic postulates to the ideologically problematic dimensions of his exposition, deviate significantly from the sexual hygienics on which scientific sexual treatises and erotic manuals emanating from the First World, and widely available in translation in Latin American bookstores, are grounded. One can venture to say that the difficulty the reader might experience in attempting to "normalize" Mattoso's discourse, in either its general erotic terms or as a declaration of personal experiences, within the context of socially respectable writing about sex is a function of the way in which the *Manual* engages in various strategies to subvert current standardized sexual practices, hetero- as well as homosexual. And by appealing to a principle of sexual health—Mattoso describes in his chronicles his experiences as a sexual podiatrist who offers his clients *shiatsu*—the *Manual* reinscribes a joyfully deviant *sexo sujo* into the dominant social code of healthy sex: sex as healthful and health as a component of institutionalized sexual behavior.

One of the fundamental points to be made about the *Manual,* a dimension of both its carnivalization of "legitimate" and "illegitimate" sex and its outrageous discursive practices, is a fundamental contradiction surrounding erotic specifics. Certainly, Mattoso's text bases its appeal to a large extent on the added outrageousness of the nonresolution of the contradictions perceived from the perspective of a "balanced" sociological treatise. From one point of view, the reader might feel compelled to go beyond the text's conjugation of pediphilia and homosexuality (as well as a number of other facets of the narrator's exercise of sex, such as its public announcement, its promiscuity, its transgressive blend of the erotic and the politically oppressive, and its transgressive blend of the erotic and the medical) and say that Mattoso's *Manual* is simply synecdochic as regards the need to promote alternative programs of sexuality, especially in the context of AIDS. (For a scholarly defense of such a proposition, see Cohen's article on Foucault, an appropriate reference point, as it was Foucault who examined the concept of sexuality as a sociopolitical, institutionalized construct. In his postface to the *Manual,* however, Perlongher underscores how Mattoso subverts the medical discourse on AIDS [175–76].) From this perspective, Mattoso liberates a series of sexual signifiers as part of a program to challenge the reader to reconsider sexual practices beyond the institutionalized, whether that institutionalization concerns the hegemonic heterosexual program or involves what he considers to be deleterious reifications of a dominant but limited range of practices within homosexuality (112–16). Such a reading, of course, will serve primarily to permit the reader to reinsert Mattoso's discourse about alternate sexuality within institutionalized practices because it sanctions the retuning of discordant elements within a generalized, and therefore nonconcretely material, concept of sexual liberation that allows one to ignore unseemly details.

Yet there is a point beyond which such an allegorical reading of the *Manual* breaks down and the novel's fundamentally outrageous nature reasserts itself in the fact that, radical dispersion of sexual signifiers aside, the narrator's discourse focuses over and over again on one form of sexual activity, the erotic pleasure to be derived from practices centered on the sucking of dirty feet (a fact that is graphically inescapable in the Glaucomix version of the text). In the process, the narrator provides a categorically accurate portrait of actual sexual desire: "Porra, como tem cara louco nesta cidade . . ." (154).[11]

This chapter has examined three narrative texts under the rubric of gay culture. It would be inappropriate for me to assert that they have a unitary stance toward this rather general concept, particularly as I have characterized Arenas's novel as marked less by a homosexual thematics than by a gay sensibility, Levi Calderón's novel as a specifically lesbian liberationist consciousness, and Mattoso's autobiography as a commitment to something like a pansexuality in which gender-based identities and acts seem trivial in the wake of strong assertions regarding transgressive sexual experimentation. Perhaps the best way of seeing these texts as contributions toward a Latin American discourse of sexuality is in terms of their variegated challenges to compulsory heterosexuality. The challenge to the latter is not so much a defense of a specific form of male or female homosexuality (*pace* the grim psychomedical connotations of that phrase) as it is a defiance of, to use Peter Fry's marvelous evocation of a colloquial Brazilian trope, sex *pra inglês ver*—the face of sex presented to the (missionary) Englishman, which means, to be sure, not only heterosexuality, but heterosexuality within the confines of passionless, functional creation. The image of the bourgeoisie in both Arenas's and Levi Calderón's novels—society in the throes of decay from within in the case of the former; society as all-too-effeciently and frighteningly functioning in the case of the latter—afford the authors with carefully articulated backdrops against which to project individuals whose personal imperatives, only synechdocally sexual, are radically deviant: the result, because a queer sensibility, is fundamentally socially deconstructive. It is for this reason that Mattoso's sexual handbook, although clearly promoting modalities of male homoeroticism, goes beyond the specifically gay, to the extent that the fetish it promotes is almost allegorically non–gender specific. Where treatises on the joys of lesbian or gay sex highlight eroneous zones and erotic activities that privilege what is either characteristically feminine or characteristically masculine, foot fetishism in Mattoso's *Manual*, aside from the possibility of associating it with a form of enslavement in the paradigmatic case of Chinese foot binding, reaches toward a gay sensibility precisely in its degendering of erotic pleasure, in its rejection of sex as masculine or feminine role playing. Much remains to be explored in these realms of Latin American cultural production, and I have chosen to content myself here with something like the act of criticism as itself metonymic or synechdocal: less the representation of particularly eloquent examples (although I think that they are) than a proposition regarding the types of material that must be looked at if we are to go beyond the merely thematic, the merely (auto)biographical in characterizing how a truly comprehensive range of erotic experiences are encoded in Latin American writing.

María Elena Walsh:
Children's Literature
and the Feminist Voice

¡Y ahora abran grandes los ojos y aparten del oído el pelo de
la patilla porque lo que sigue es absolutamente maravilloso y
no van a encontrarlo en otro cuento así como así.

—Walsh, *Chaucha y palito*

En esta calle, señores,
todo el mundo mire bien,
que aquí pasan muchas cosas
pero muy pocas se ven.

—Walsh, *El reino del revés*

A radical theory of children's literature must determine how
the subjects of children's literature—children—become less
real images of real children but images of subject children,
ideologically constructed to reflect or subvert the hegemonic
practices of a ruling class.

—Phillips and Wojcik-Andrews

The term *children's literature* is a virtual oxymoron in Western culture. Despite multiple vanguard redefinitions and the onslaughts of
a presumed postmodernist sensibility, literature as a pivotal concept
of culture, even if it is no longer restricted to high sectors, remains
persuasively operant. This is so whether on the one hand it is viewed

(like most of culture) as a means of escaping an all-too-omnipresent social reality or as a complex series of reinscriptions of the social text toward enabling its beneficent reconstitution. In either case, literature has ascribed to it an enormous power that explains in part why its privileged domain continues to resist dissolution (see Hunt for an excellent discussion of the critical and theoretical parameters of a children's literature).

By the same token, the vast increase in literacy in this century and its extension to the youngest possible sectors of our society mean that works for children are vital. A specific publication market for children goes hand-in-hand with the reification of the concept of childhood; and the multiplication of diverse stages of childhood, the postulation of transitional phases, the linking of childhood to adulthood via other psychobiological periods, such as adolescence, the preteen years, or young adulthood, all abet the proliferation of specialized writing. Moreover, much as purists might lament the displacement of books by other forms of pre-adult culture, it takes no great effort to demonstrate how book publishing is intimately tied into and supported by movies, television, songs, and assorted forms of graphic media.

What is problematical—what is, in fact, oxymoronic—about the term *children's literature* is the virtual noncoextensiveness of the domain of children's writing with the aforementioned spectrum of literature, in whatever shadings one might wish to accord it. We can speak of writing for children as belonging to at least three primary categories. The first encompasses those texts that are of a prevailingly commercial nature, typically those that, like the Disney productions, tie in with a universe of high-earnings cultural production. Although it might be difficult, and perhaps even elitist, to attempt to fix definitively the frontiers of such a production, let us say that these are the sorts of books for children that are not likely to be found in an elementary-education curriculum library or in any children's collection developed along pedagogical principles (it may simply be that it is assumed children will have access elsewhere to this production, and it is up to a professional library science to provide alternate, less universalized examples of culture).

Of course, one would want to underscore how these highly commercialized books must necessarily touch on the escapist function of literature, either because they configure worlds that are radically disjunctive with any degree of an acknowledged social reality (e.g., monster stories, sensationalist science fiction, sentimentalized Westerns, all usually colored by stereotypic forms of violence) or because they represent images of a recognizable social reality that is, nevertheless, interpreted in ways that cannot withstand the slightest sociologically principled examination (e.g., anthropocentric animal stories, Dick-and-Jane idealizations, and, again, sentimentalized Westerns). At the same time, one cannot deny that this broad array does not exercise some function of socialization, no matter how much some might be loathe to acknowledge it. There have been several key studies on the sort of normative social world figured by traditional Walt Disney texts, studies that underscore how such a normalization must be effected by dramatically contradicting social reality in a process of (false, it is alleged) utopian construction that must come at great cost to collective consciousness and that, if it is effective, as it often seems to be on the sheer basis of its sales, bespeaks enormously skillful discourse practices on the part of its producers (see, e.g., Dorfman and Mattelart).

Social normalization here may not necessarily mean the incorporation by the individual of an image of the world that is "really" like that of Donald Duck; it is enough for the reader to prefer to contemplate Donald Duck's world for the discourse practices that produce it to be deemed awesomely effective. This is especially notable when one considers the transformation of authentic or legendary folkloric material, which presumably is a productive inscription of a verifiable social reality, into mass commercial culture: the distance between the precommercial tradition of, say, Snow White and the Disney et al. presentation of it does not separate social normalization from its suspension, but marks two very different processes of social normalization. Thus in this formulation, we can say that even the most dreck and dross varieties of commercial children's literature play a role in the process of socialization, and one must pause to consider that the degree of effective socialization may well be in direct proportion to the level of exploitative reiteration of semiotic schema, precisely because what is well known achieves effective reenforcement.

A second category of children's writing, which includes major

María Elena Walsh

components of the material that a curriculum-based library collection is likely to stock, involves texts that are somehow inscribed in a process of social awareness, consciousness raising, the reconfiguration of values, or the depiction of a realm of the unknown that is judged to involve a vital interest. This text production assumes the function of literature, especially for children, to be predicated primarily on a process of social normalization, although the social norms being displayed may not be those of the prevailing standard. It is for this reason that literature under this purview usually matches the prevailing liberal agenda, although there is no reason not to believe, in contexts that may be at some times more limited but at others attain a majority primacy, that such a production may not match a conservative, or even a reactionary, agenda. The point is not their locus on the popularly understood political spectrum, but rather the fact that they give prominence and precedence to the goal of social formation and normalization: the revival of a mid-nineteenth century "McGuffey's reader" tradition on the one hand and the need to address questions of racial equality, ethnic pride, women's rights, and the like on the other exemplify what I am talking about.

Yet as controversial as the process of consciousness raising may be for some of this writing, it is actually quite conservative, tame, or restricted in its understanding of the possibilities of figuring alternate social domains, because in general it adheres to something like a principle of reformism: nothing like a reconfiguration of social reality, but a more sensitive recognition of it, and usually in only its most benevolent dimensions. Or, to put it differently, the spheres of utopianism that may be said to constitute one way in which literature as a manifestation of cultural production in a society legitimates itself are not present in any significant way in this type of writing.

It is such a lack that renders the term children's literature oxymoronic. Although one can point to some manifestations of a "radical writing" for children—or, at least, a radical writing that uses the semiotic formats and morphology of children's writing, although it may be directed to or consumed by adults—such a production is not characteristic of the mainstream of children's literature and may even be considered antithetical to it. Yet it is such a circumstance that marginalizes children's literature from the realm of otherwise comprehensive literary studies. The latter may on occasion discover texts of this ilk and afford them treatment as coequals with "serious" adult production. But this attention only serves to inscribe a minimal segment of children's writing within the orbit of adult literature, while either ignoring what is, in fact, generally produced for children or failing to attribute any notable distinction to what is examined, beyond saying that it seems to be written for children but satisfies the interests of adult readers. The literature in this category one has in mind often includes texts written for children by important mainline literary figures, as is the case with the series Amelia Hannois directed in the early 1970s, which included original texts in Spanish by Silvina Ocampo, Griselda Gambaro, Augusto Roa Bastos, and Fernando Alegría; and translations into Spanish of texts by Umberto Eco, Eugène Ionesco, Ray Bradbury, Clarice Lispector, and Michel Butor.

A distinguishing mark of such writing is, however, not so much the ability to read it in conformance with the practices of adult literature, although it is certainly a question of attributing to the writers a desire to take writing for children seriously. Rather, what one needs to consider is the possibility of attributing to this category of writing a second level of meaning that, nevertheless, retains an emphasis on a reading audience of the young. In an immediate way, one would be correct to assume that the texts being discussed at this moment are responding to an imperative to make use of writing directed at children for purposes of consciousness raising, for the advancement of a specifically ethical understanding of society, and for the general formation of values that echo a sense of the betterment of the human community. The texts at issue confirm a progressive function for culture, much in the same way that the bulk of "professional" children's writing does.

Yet there is a second level to this type of text production, one that escapes easy classification in terms of a typology of professional children's writing. It is most immediately evident in a form of children's writing that promotes a sense of the fantastic, of the magically real, or of the absurd in ways that may even constitute a challenge to the enlightened knowledge promoted by the second category proposed above: it is challenging to the extent that it seems to replace a liberal criterion of *expanded* knowledge with a more radical one of *restructured* knowledge. It can be said that the latter is paradigmatically represented by production under the aegis of Sesame Street—thoroughly educational texts with a twist of just enough of the outrageous both to hold the reader's attention and to undermine beliefs (e.g., female dependency) that enough of the populace is willing to revise, serving the agenda of liberal consciousness raising. At the same time, it is thoroughly instructional in the areas of primary knowledge (numbers, letters, colors, shapes, etc.).

The third category of children's writing is made up of texts that for many adult readers are threatening precisely to the degree that they move beyond the need to provide primary instruction and the confirmation of a beneficent social awareness. One thinks immediately of the concern provoked by the books of Maurice Sendak, especially his *Where the Wild Things Are* (1964), which was felt to provoke terror in children but was fascinating for its recognition of the so-called dark side of human nature as it is present in the young (something adults can acceptably read about in a novel such as William Golding's *Lord of the Flies,* but which they may feel children are not yet ready to contemplate). Shel Silverstein's poetry, such as *Where the Sidewalk Ends* (1974), likewise promotes a sort of subversive knowledge about the instability of human existence that clearly defies any sort of requirement that children's culture must, à la Beatrix Potter, socialize its audience into an ordered and transparently meaningful sense of life. Or one might even mention the Dr. Seuss books, which certainly have had their ardent detractors over the years. Seuss's anarchic liberties with the English language are upsetting to those who regard the establishment of language as a fixed code characterized by the bidirectional relationship between form and meaning and the need for that relationship to be securely imprinted in the mind of the child at as early an age as possible. Language is considered to be the master code of human society in general, as well as of specific societies as recognizable communities. It is for this reason that we can understand how the Seuss oeuvre has been known to provoke an alarmist reaction among those who subscribe to a conservative functionalism of language as the master code. Such a functionalism tends to hold the view that challenges to language stability of any sort (but apparently especially semantic) portend all sorts of psycho- and sociolinguistic problems for individuals and their society.

All of these works may be in one way or another integrated over time in a vanguard of children's literature—certainly Seuss is now a veritable icon of the movement away from the Dick-and-Jane tradition, a movement all but the diehard agree has been necessary to the extent that that tradition only served to turn young readers away from the printed page. But there always exists the possibility of examining this third category of texts as fundamentally subversive, as essentially challenging in a dramatic way one or another received concepts regarding children, whether it be the way they learn and organize language, their sense of the meaning of life, their perception of a threatening dimension to human existence, or any number of processes related to their interaction with the symbolic norms socialization through culture is viewed as providing them. Alison Lurie has, in fact, made a point about the fundamentally subversive dimensions of a broad array of children's literature in her eloquently titled *Don't Tell the Grown-ups: Subversive Children's Literature:*

> Most of the great works of juvenile literature are subversive in one way or another: they express ideas and emotions not generally approved of or even recognized at the time; they make fun of honored figures and piously held beliefs; and they view social pretenses with clear-eyed directness, remarking—as in Andersen's famous tale—that the emperor has no clothes. (4)

There is another point to be made about the constitution of children's writing: the role of the woman author. Although there may have been in recent decades serious reversals in the conception of elementary education as an extension of the home and the primacy of the female elementary teacher as a maternal surrogate (the objection to male elementary teachers has as much to do with this principle as it does with the idea of the male as a potential sexual predator, and the longstanding demand that schoolmarms be unmarried virgins served to invest them, in a predominantly Protestant and lay society, with a nunlike vocation as surrogate mothers), Western society continues to associate with elementary education the presence of women, if for no other reason than a continued economic exploitation of the female teacher. I do not know what the statistical distribution of male versus female writers of children's literature is, especially as this writing is characterized by the use of pseudonyms. Yet there is no question that someone such as Beatrix Potter left an indelible mark on children's writing as a cultural genre to which women could make especially valuable contributions, an undertaking that can in one way be understood as of a whole with the Lacanian hypothesis concerning the fundamental socializing role of women in transmitting the patriarchal symbolic norms.

Thus one would expect to find women writers who play an integral role in the composition of a normalizing children's literature to be particularly noteworthy when they set aside this canonical function and write texts that can be viewed as proposing subversive configurations of the social realm.

María Elena Walsh (1930) is just such an author, and what is remarkable about her is that an initial examination of her extensive production of poetry for children places her squarely within the tradition of the female children's author.[1] By this I mean that her poetry, in more than a dozen published volumes, repeats many of the time-honored practices of children's writing: (1) the emphasis on anthropomorphized animals (a tradition that Walt Disney merely exploited and transformed, but did not invent, in that the Mother Goose convention is firmly entrenched in the Western tradition and, indeed, is to be found in similar manifestations almost on a universal culture level), (2) the use of traditional rhyming meters in sing-song formats that allow both for easy memory and musical instrumentalization (Walsh has published several recordings in which she sings her poems to her own guitar accompaniment, and she has pursued a self-image as La Juglaresa de Buenos Aires), and (3) the implied conviction that writing for children performs a socializing function in the teaching of social manners, interpersonal ethics, and a general understanding of how the world works.

Although it may be argued that the latter is, indeed, the function of all culture (cf. the famous New Criticism premise that literature is "education for living"), nonchildren's literature may not necessarily be sustained by a commitment to the integration of the reader into neighborly social norms and, more significantly, it is customarily marked by features of uncompromising analysis, including ambiguity, irony, revisionism, and the like, absent from the "straightforward" social semantics of writing directed at children. Put differently, it would be difficult to argue for any trace of a seditious, contestatorial, or countercultural positing in Walsh's poetry or short fiction. Indeed, the two dominant marks of her writing, the Seussian wordplay and the sense of the absurd, the topos of "el mundo al revés," are unproblematical extensions of conventions well established, if not in Spanish-language children's writing, in the sort of internationalist bibliography that Argentine children routinely have access to in translations from English and other Western languages (concerning the use of colloquial language in Walsh, see Pagni).

What, then, should one look for as particularly distinctive in Walsh's writing, especially within the context of a feminist commitment? I would propose that significant transition in Walsh's literature from conventional writing by a woman for children—understanding that we must leave open the question as to whether that writing is irremediably patriarchal and whether there is not some element of social reconfiguration necessarily present by virtue of the feminine voice—lies in two directions: (1) a resemanticization of certain paradigmatic female roles, such as teacher, guardian/protector, old maid, and repository of manifestations of social margination to be pitied or lamented; and (2) a compelling argument for the acceptance of the socially different, something like a strategic recasting of the Ugly Duckling motif and the plea for the acceptance of the physically deviant.

I would like to initiate an illustration of this potential in Walsh's writing with a discussion of three poems from *Tutú Marambá* that deal with the figure of Doña Disparate. The figure of the eccentric, especially of the eccentric female, is a staple of patriarchal writing, and it bespeaks all of the reservations in the sectors of social control for those individuals—the "wild outcasts"—who threaten social stability less by any overt attack upon its institution than by the deleterious example of being less than completely assimilated to them. Such figures constitute the stress points of a social organization because they exemplify zones, practices, or relations that are problematical to the extent that there is the possibility of an nonconformity or an inadaptability to them. Typically, eccentric old women, whether as harmless old dears (Old Mother Hubbard) or as outcast wicked witches of the East and West, are, if not objects of discomfort and fear, objects of derision.

In "El perrito loquito" (The Crazy Dog; 49–50), Walsh undertakes a frank adaptation of the Old Mother Hubbard motif. But whereas in the traditional English text the dithery old lady's concern is over feeding her poor dog, in Walsh's text the animal becomes a trigger for her hysterical catering to his wants. That is, the eccentric concern over a domestic animal translates into the need to involve the world at large in every effort on his behalf, although the dog's behavior at every point contradicts or undermines her concern for him, as though somehow it were irrelevant. The lack of real-world logical connection between her ministrations and the dog's needs underscores her eccentricity and only leads, spiralling, to her ever greater hysteria, marked by a pattern of lexical *accumulatio:*

Doña Disparate corre, salta y vuela
por las avenidas, llamando al doctor,
pero cuando llega su perro se muere
con el rabo tieso y el ombligo al sol.

Doña Disparate llama a los bomberos,
a la policía y al sastre y al cura,
pero cuando llegan todos, el perrito
está muy contento bailando la rumba. . . .

Doña Disparate sigue disparando
con cuarenta diablos en las zapatillas,
mientras el perrito se queda en la casa,
sentado tranquilo fumando la pila. (50)[2]

It is evident that this text does not go beyond the characterization of the woman as a silly old lady whose exaggerated running about seems to be almost mischievously provoked by her pet.

Another poem, "Desastres" (Disasters; 63–64), is also built around a series of microincidents, this time having to do with five outrageous desires she has. Each stanza describes the desire, describes her foolish attempt to attain it, and the subsequent frustration of that desire. Each stanza concludes with a coda whose use of repeated words or phrases emphasizes Doña Disparate's eccentricity:

> Doña Disparate va a buscar un bicho
> que vive en un árbol muy alto, muy alto.
> Se quiebra la rama, y la vieja pícara
> ¡patapúm! se cae sentada en un charco.
> Se cae sentada, sentada en un charco. (64)[3]

This stanza is especially noteworthy in its adherence to the violence that has customarily been described as a dominant feature of the Mother Goose cycle, in which the intense physical sufferings of a creature's existence are translated into an almost nonchalant litany of contusions, lacerations, and the like. Doña Disparate literally pays for each one her desires in a humiliating manner, and in this instance with bodily harm. In any case, in none of the five attempts does she attain her foolish goal.

But it is another text, titled simply "Doña Disparate" (Mrs. Crazy Thing; 73–74) in which Walsh dramatically revises the topos of the silly old lady (it is important to note how the three texts are spaced out every ten pages beginning in the middle of the book). Eight stanzas of foreshortened meter provide pithy descriptions of the woman's nonconformist behavior: in clinical terms one would be tempted to describe her as basically a victim of something like Alzheimer's disease. In each case, the woman's conduct is either behaviorly or constitutively inappropriate of an implied social norm:

No sabe, no sabe,
y aprieta un botón
para que haya luna
o se apague el sol.

Oye con el diente,
habla con la oreja,
con un cucharón
barre la vereda. (73)[4]

Here the recital of quirks attributed to Doña Disparate is much more pointed than in the case of the previous poems: in "El perro loquito," the woman only runs about wildly as she misses the mark in ministering to her dog, whereas in "Desastres" she is seen as embarked on a number of outrageous quests that are, nevertheless, not of a specifically constitutional nature. In "Doña Disparate," however, the woman's acts go directly to the core of primary social norms, such as knowing one's communitarian identity, using correctly the agencies of commerce, and grasping the established connection between instruments and causes. All of these norms are considerably weakened, if not abolished or distorted, in the case of this text's Doña Disparate.

Yet what is distinctive about this text is the sudden double insertion of the authorial voice:

Doña Disparate,
nariz de merengue,
se "ecovica," digo,
se equivoca siempre. (74)[5]

The narrator appears with the tag "digo," whose person marker identifies categorically the provenance of the text from a specific individual identity, an intrusion that always serves to remind the reader of a text that the semantic configuration, the existential interpretations, the value judgments all have their origin in a subjective locus that is the originator of what is being read as a structured explication of human affairs.

But what is more significant is the actual meaning of "digo" in this context. Coming as a transitional tag between two propositions, *se ecovica* and *se equivoca,* the phrase here means "rather, what I mean is" or "that is to say." In short, it is used by the speaker to correct an erroneous statement by introducing what was meant to be said. The implication of this is that it is not only Doña Disparate who is responsible for *disparates,* but the narrator herself. The form *ecovica* is a "dumb mistake," the metathesis of two syllables in a basic lexical item such as *equivocarse* (to make a mistake, to get things wrong), and it is the sort of aphasic mistake made not by a skilled poet but by someone who is in less than optimal control of the language. That is to say, Walsh here suddenly puts her own poetic discourse on the same level as Doña Disparate's language. The latter may be a generalized loss of control over language and the reality it purportedly serves to encode, whereas Walsh's closure is a momentary slip—and one that, after all, is only a clever rhetorical figure.

However, by assimilating, at the close of her poem, her own voice to Doña Disparate's generalized "problem," Walsh implies certainly not a degradation of her poetic discourse but something like a vindication of Doña Disparate, the silly old woman, the figure of the marginalized aged female. As a woman, and as a mature, single, childless female (cf. her declarations in "El cuento de la autora" 166 [The author's story]), Walsh is herself subject to the same social discriminations to which the Doña Disparates of our society fall victim, and it is for this reason that this rather unusual discursive intersubjectivity that serves as a coda to the poem is especially noteworthy.

Walsh is mostly known for her poetry, but she has also written a number of short stories for children. The bulk of this writing adheres to the general characteristics of her lyrics, especially in the reliance on images of anthropomorphized animals and in the privileging of a symbiotic relationship between solitary or marginalized human beings, paradigmatically but exclusively children (cf. in particular the collection *Chaucha y Palito*)[6] and animals, some of which may also be to one degree or another outcasts. One of Walsh's most carefully wrought texts, and one with especially prominent sociopolitical implications, involves precisely such an interaction.

La sirena y el capitán (The Siren and the Captain), a story published as a single book, centers on a siren: "Había una vez una sirena que vivía por el río Paraná. Tenía un ranchito de hojas en un camalote y allí pasaba los días peinando su largo pelo color de ébano, y pasaba las noches cantando porque su oficio era cantar" (2).[7] Alahí is less of an example of the merger of the intermingling of the animal and the human in Walsh's narrative world than she is emblematic of a unified, prelapsarian nature: she is a female figure, the focal point of an Edenic pre-Columbian Latin America (in which, to be sure, the Río Paraná was not yet named the Río Paraná and Latin America was not yet Latin America, but such are the conventions of literature) in which all of nature is in harmonious balance under the tutelage of her song: "Hasta los [animales] que parecían más malos, como los caimanes y las víboras, se le acercaban mimosos" (4).[8] Walsh's text, therefore, postulates an overdetermined semantic cluster around the figure of Alahí that the reader presumably understands as the prelapsarian condition of Latin America supported by a bispecies female songstress of the greater harmony of an integrated nature: "Hace muchos años de esto. América todavía era india y no habían llegado los españoles con sus barbas y sus barcos" (6).[9]

But, of course, the Spaniards do arrive, and what they bring with them is a planned exploitation of the Edenic New World: "Soy marinero y aventurero, vengo de España y olé. Quiero gloria, quiero dinero y con los dos volveré" (7).[10] Alahí becomes a sign of the rare wealth of the Americas, and the Spanish captain tries to make her his wife and take her back to Spain. When she resists, he punishes her by tying her to a tree (in a typical pathetic fallacy, all of nature weeps for her entrapment). In a synecdochal gesture of the conqueror's destruction of nature, the Spaniard begins to chop down a tree in order to make a chest in which to hold Alahí prisoner. But the siren's fellow denizens of unspoiled nature rise up in unison to protect her: they attack the captain, drive him and his crew away in fright, and free the victim from her bonds:

—¡Gracias, amigos, gracias por este regalo, el más hermoso para mí: la libertad!

Amanecía cuando la sirena volvió a su camalote, escoltada por cielo y tierra de todos sus amigos. Allá muy lejos se iba el barco de los hombres extraños.

Alahí tomó el rumbo contrario en su camalote y se alejó río arriba, hasta Paitití, el país de la leyenda, donde sigue viviendo libre y cantando siempre para quien sepa oírla. (19)[11]

Characterized by a rigorous series of binary disjunctions, *La sirena y el capitán* leaves little doubt as to the opposition between an idyllic nature and the forces that threaten it, the importance of music as a metonym of that nature and the raucous noise of the invaders, and the paradigmatic roles of a woman as a sign of natural integration and an oafish man who, in a caricature of patriarchal prerogatives, undertakes to exploit it.

On the one hand, Walsh's text is historical in that it does relate, if in a particularly harsh Manichaean way, the circumstances of, as the current Spanish government likes to put it, the encounter between two cultures. Furthermore, it is unquestionably ideological in the sense that the binary oppositions it marshals are resolutely unambiguous in portraying the Spaniards as vile masculine destroyers (with the inescapable implication for the "advanced" reader of the literal violation of Alahí as a necessary preliminary to the rape of American nature) and a feminine American nature, where there is a highly charged symbolic underdifferentiation of the species as somehow indicative of a pre-Fall Eden, as a harmonious utopia. The text's factoring out of a negative constellation of male traits and a positive constellation of female ones, accompanied by an especially eloquent and significant conjoining of the feminine and the poetic, may not resist anything like a subtle sociocultural analysis. However, one does not demand subtle shades of meaning from children's stories, and, indeed, such stark disjunctions are well within the discourse conventions of texts like Walsh's (one only need think of the innumerable oppositions between Good and Evil in, say, the Disney oeuvre).

MARÍA ELENA WALSH

Yet *La sirena y el capitán* departs radically from the historical interpretation it seems so dramatically to suggest, because, as any knowledgeable reader (but not necessarily the children to whom it is ostensibly addressed) will have realized, the Spaniards did *not* depart the New World, American nature did *not* remain harmoniously integrated (whatever that notion means), suprareal icons like Alahí did *not* escape the violence of the conquerors, and her voice is, in fact, *not* to be heard in the legendary realm of Paitití. None of this means to imply, however, that Walsh's text is guilty of false consciousness, nor that it suddenly becomes transformed into a piece of antihistorical fantasy. Rather, what seems to be at issue here is something like a utopian configuration: not the falsification of history but the imagining of a domain of Latin American identity where, in fact, Alahí can still be said to be alive and well and singing, if only on the levels of poetic consciousness Walsh's literature pretends to have access to. Thus the operant discourse practice here is not to belie history, not to pretend it didn't happen, but to touch those reaches of the Latin American experience in which the process set in motion by history has not yet completely wiped away the potential for maintaining/retaining/recovering a sense of harmonious integration with nature where Alahí is a palpable reality "para quien sepa oírla."

From the perspective of the reader familiar with the enormously complex readings of Latin American history encoded in narratives such as *Cien años de soledad* and an entire cultural production since the 1960s that offers interpretations, in various Marxist versions, of the continent's history, *La sirena y el capitán* as somehow a prototype of ecofeminism is decidedly facile. But then it would be inappropriate to require that a narrative written for children aspire to the level of complexity of García Márquez's novel, and it would certainly be even more inappropriate to suggest that the literature of someone like Walsh not attempt to provide its readers with historical interpretations within its own conventional practices.

One of the venerable topoi of poetry is the confession of expressive inadequacy. Although the claim is frequently made for the special knowledge provided by poetry and for the vatic role of the poet who possesses abilities to lead us to perceive reality in new ways, the confession of expressive inadequacy is a countervailing force that underscores the tentativeness of all human endeavor, including the codes of natural language. True, the topoi of inadequacy enjoys a variety of functions, many of them ironic (false humility, for example) or figures of exaggeration: the event or experience to be recounted is so profound that it outstrips the potential of poetry and the capacity of the individual poet; the result is that our admiration for the awesome that the poet is able to communicate is enhanced. Or the topoi may simply be used as a convenient way to close a text: the poet, overcome by the task at hand, cannot go on.

This interplay between the alleged privileged knowledge provided by poetry and strategic recognitions of expressive inadequacy is intimately bound with traditional beliefs in Western culture about the immanence of meaning and the authoritarian primacy of language as the master code of social interaction. Concomitantly, the perception that the discourse practices of our culture in addition to being dominantly authoritarian are fundamentally masculinist and that, in effect, authoritarianism and masculinism are one and the same thing is essential to most varieties of contemporary feminism. It may be an open question whether the structural design of language is inherently and necessarily authoritarian vis-à-vis the relationship between form and function or whether the sort of issues Derrida's grammatology examines are simply the consequence of how otherwise neutral language structure is deployed by a patriarchal society. The fact remains that our culture functions with a firmly entrenched linguistic ideology whereby "words mean what they mean," "you've got to say what you mean," and "tell me clearly what you've got to say." Certain poetics may underscore the essential ambiguity of language (e.g., Anglo-American New Criticism), but such proposals do not modify the hegemonic cultural belief in the transparency of language and the need to both recognize and promote its validity in nonpoetic contexts.

Walsh does not, aside from word play in general and examples of irony, concern herself much with the question of the problematics of meaning (it is quite another matter whether her "adult" poetry may be fruitfully examined for manifestations of an *écriture feminine*).[12] Where she does evince an interest in the possibility of deconstructing the normative demands of linguistic expression are those occasions in which she plays with the conventions of narrative discourse, as though defying the imperative to be coherent. Certainly, Walsh's texts in general are marked by the playful inventiveness I have examined elsewhere ("Playful Ecphrasis"), and there are considerable examples in her texts of the defiance of compositional practices that yield a diversity of interpretive possibilities, only one major one of which would be the undermining of an authoritarian conception of narrative logic. Such is exemplified by the poem "Voy a contar un cuento" (I'm Going to Tell a Story) (*El reino del revés* 11–14), which is truly metanarrative in nature, to the extent that nothing ever really gets told except for the self-confessed aphasic confusion, a variant of the topos of expressive inadequacy, of the narrator:

> Voy a contar un cuento.
> A la una, a las dos, y a las tres:
> Había una vez.
>
> ¿Cómo sigue después? (11) [13]

The rhetorical question triggers the fundamental conditions of the poem's narrative logic: the inability to recall and state correctly the details of the story being told. Statements to the effect that information is unknown or has been forgotten and that she cannot remember which fact is the correct one are complemented by the obligation to correct what has already been said, as well as by declarations that she has lost track of her place in the story:

> El Marqués era malo, le pegó con un palo
> a . . . No, el Marqués no fue.
> Me equivoqué.
>
> No importa. Sigo. . . .
>
> Después pasaba algo
> que no recuerdo bien.
> Quizás pasaba el tren . . .

Y entonces.

Me perdí. (12–13)[14]

After going on in this vein for more than fifty lines, the narrator abruptly closes her narration under the following pretext:

Mejor que acabe ya.
Creo que a mí también
me llama mi mamá. (14)[15]

This declaration is a relatively original variant of the topos of expressive inadequacy, in that by reducing herself to the level of a child, she in effect denies herself legitimacy, according to the literatus, by virtue of a certain age and sociocultural formation: the poem assigns itself the attributes of the idle, if not infuriating, chatter of a child who does not really deserve attention.

But, of course, Walsh's text does demand attention on the basis of the contextualization of its publication and on the basis of how we are likely to understand that the narrator is really Walsh's poetic persona pretending to be a talkative but not very informative child (there is no linguistic marker on which to base a sexual designation). I venture to suggest that Walsh is not interested in capturing the qualities of a childish poetic interpretation of experience, in conformance with a proposition that children may be the ultimate vatic speakers (the stories in *Cuentopos de Gulubú* do imply something like a superior childlike experience that puts them in contact with realms most adults have lost touch with). Instead, Walsh's narrative incoherence may profitably be viewed as a parody of the rigors of expository logic with a conception of linguistic transparency and the primacy of explanation. In whatever way the latter may be identified with the masculinist project, it is possible to undertake an examination of the transgressive elements in Walsh's use of language on many levels, but in this case on that of discourse logic, as participating to one degree or another in feminist contestatorial practices. This may be seen in other recent texts, such as the following, in which the string of indicative appositions is contradicted by two

semantically negative predicates—one "almost" and the other absolute—that would, if promoted to the head position of the poetic
proposition, require subjunctive dependencies:

> Un Canario que ladra si está triste,
> que come cartulina en vez de alpiste,
> que se pasea en coche
> y toma sol de noche,
> estoy casi seguro que no existe. (*Zoo loco* 5) [16]

Once one sees the morphosyntactic effect of beginning the text with
the declaration "Estoy casi seguro de que no existe un canario que"
(I'm almost certain a canary does not exist that; i.e., *ladra, come, se
pasea* and *toma* would all have to be converted into their subjunctive
forms), it becomes necessary to ask what is being presented here:
either the nonexistence of something that is presented as existing,
along with four defining appositions, or the existence of something
that is declared almost certainly not to exist. Neither proposition,
much less the linguistic organization of its vehicle, adheres to much
of astandard of narrative coherence.

I am not claiming here that one ought to carefully reread Walsh's
literary works written for children as majors feminist statements,
nor that there is any specific form of feminist *écriture* involved
(which no longers seems to be much of a possibility anyway; see
Felski passim). That would make the task of literary criticism too
easy; moreover, Walsh has elsewhere expressed reservations concerning certain overly popularized versions of feminism (cf. her
poem "Las feministas" [The Feminists] in her collection of "adult"
texts, *Cancionero contra el mal de ojo* [Songbook against the Evil
Eye]). Indeed, it would undoubtedly be more conventional criticism
to examine her excellent production not addressed to children as
fully cogent feminist statements: "Réquiem de madre" (Mother's
Requiem), "Tejedoras" (Knitters), "Los hermafroditas" (The Her-
maphrodites), "Orquesta de señoritas" (Ladies Orchestra), "Eva
[Perón]," and "Educación sexual" (Sexual Education) are all texts in
Cancionero that suggest themselves on the most immediate level of

their titles as fruitful points of departure. Nevertheless, Walsh's principal fame is for texts such as *El reino del revés* and *Zoo loco* (Crazy Zoo). Moreover, Hispanic scholarship cannot continue to underestimate the value of writing for children as an important venue of sociocultural encounter. What I have attempted to demonstrate in this chapter is that these texts, despite whatever conventionality there may be regarding some of their superficial features, represent spheres of cultural production in which issues of feminist interest are raised and dealt with (a feminist dimension does not appear to be part of Sánchez Lihón's imperative agenda for a Latin American children's literature).

Perhaps neither the execution nor the conclusion manifests the complex textuality associated with, say, Griselda Gambaro or Alejandra Pizarnik, to cite two Argentine writers who have attracted particularly distinguished feminist readings. But if children's literature is addressed to individuals at a time when the formation of their sociocultural parameters is both especially vulnerable and advantageously receptive, a little bit of ideological signification may, in fact, go quite a long way: "Ustedes me dirán qué tiene que ver una cosa con la otra . . ." (*Chaucha y Palito* 35).[17] Or, as Walsh also says to her readers: "Son ustedes que terminarán de modificar [el mundo]" ("El cuento de la autora" 166).[18]

It is striking to note that, given the importance of key figures such María Walsh in Argentina and Gloria Fuertes in Spain, there has been scant critical attention in the Spanish language devoted to writing for children (I am purposefully overlooking here didactic material such as Pastoriza de Etchebarne), much less any sustained theorizing. For this reason, one must inevitably turn toward non-Hispanic models, especially the extensive tradition in English; even a work such as Dorfman's *Empire's Old Clothes*, which makes reference to children's literature, is actually not concerned with Spanish-language texts but the consumption in Latin America of translations of foreign texts and the consumption through them of abiding imperialist models. *Puro cuento*'s interview with Walsh is entitled "El cuento infantil no entra en el Parnaso," and this attitude toward children's writing as a subgenre translates into critical and theoretical inattention, which in the case of Walsh is rendered suspect precisely because of the enormous readership among children, as well as adults, her stories and her poems/songs have enjoyed. I propose that her writing is perhaps one of the best places in Latin American literature to begin the enormous task of surveying this production and rendering an adequate interpretive account of it.

ARGENTINE JEWISH DRAMATISTS:
ASPECTS OF A NATIONAL CONSCIOUSNESS

One of the most outstanding features of Argentine social and cultural history is the fact that Argentina—at least that majority of Argentina that is concentrated in the Buenos Aires and littoral region—is essentially an immigrant nation. Although facile comparisons between Argentina and the United States are certainly inappropriate—whereas the United States has developed as a pluralistic society, Argentina has tended to subjugate immigrant and ethnically and racially marginal elements to a dominant creole-Hispanic culture—immigration to the two countries occurred roughly during the same period, drew people from many of the same areas of Western and Eastern Europe, and faced many of the same problems and tensions occasioned by social transformations that were impossible to foretell.

Like the United States, Argentina became home to many Jewish immigrants, second in number only to Italians, who provide the bulk of names in Buenos Aires today; certainly Argentina's Jewish community is presently the largest in Latin America (Elkin, *Jews;* Elkin, "A Demographic Profile"). This immigration is a story that has been told many times, often in highly romanticized terms, often in a very fragmentary fashion, and the bibliography on the subject is understandably quite extensive (cf. Weisbrot for the most comprehensive survey; also Sofer). Argentine-Jewish writers and intellectuals have made significant contributions to national culture, especially since 1930, when the children and grandchildren of the immigrant influx that began around 1880 moved into positions of influence in major areas of national life. Many Argentine Jews have left Argentina in recent decades, however, because of continuing turmoil in the country, which includes the sporadic and disturbing persecution of minority sectors of society—the case of Jacobo Timerman is, of course, but the most internationally visible incident. Despite the intense controversy surrounding his person and views, Timerman's book cannot be ignored as a significant Argentine sociocultural document. Significantly, Timerman dedicates his book to Rabbi Marshall Meyer, the American who serves as Chief Rabbi in Buenos Aires and who worked tirelessly on behalf of Argentines who suffered human rights violations during the 1976–1983 military dictatorships. The *Latin American Report,* a publication of the Anti-Defamation League of B'nai B'rith, for July 1984 states flatly: "Anti-Semitism remains a grave problem for Jews in Argentina even though the democratic government of President Raúl Alfonsín is sympathetic to Jewish concerns" (1). But Argentina continues to be characterized by an exceptionally high level of participation by members of the *colectividad judía* in all spheres of cultural and intellectual endeavor (Liebman; Diament; Sebreli). Such participation has been particularly noteworthy in literature, including drama and the theater.

A notable amount of recent scholarship has dealt with literature by Argentine Jews and the Jewish experience. Leonardo Senkman surveys in considerable detail a wide array of authors, and the additional names he might have included testify to the importance of this ethnic category of Argentine letters (Senkman). Saúl Sosnowski has been engaged in an interpretation of the most significant literary versions of Argentine and Latin American Jewish life, and several installments of his project have appeared. Naomi Lindstrom has recently completed a monograph providing the most complete literary analysis of Argentine-Jewish writings to date (Lindstrom, *Argentine-Jewish Writers*). Lindstrom argues for the need to provide satisfactory literary analyses of these works, rather than thematic and sociopolitcally reductionist commentaries, in her "Problems and Possibilities in the Analysis of Jewish Argentine Literary Works," a series of proposals dealing with the problems of studying as literary texts works that are initially identified for their status as ethnic and cultural testimonies (see also Schwartz; Sadow; Goodman). Although many of the aforementioned scholars refer to dramatic works, there has been little in the way of specific analysis of theatrical traditions (cf. Kleiner; Schallman). Yet it is in the theater that Jewish writers and artists made their earliest and more concentrated impact. Again like the United States, Argentina had an early and flourishing theater in Yiddish (Weisbrot 103–4; Sandrow 87–90 and 373–76; "Yiddish Theater"). This theater constituted a vital manifestation of the culture of the Jewish community during the early decades of immigration. By the 1930s, Jewish dramatists had begun to make the decisive transition from works in Yiddish to works in Spanish. As a consequence, Jewish dramatists, directors, and actors emerged as an important component of the Teatro Independiente movement, which spanned the three decades between 1930 and 1960. This movement, which attempted to revitalize the Argentine stage through a program of noncommercial theatrical activity involving both the "education" of those connected with all aspects of theatrical production and the theater public in a manner roughly equivalent to New York's off-Broadway theater, was significant in the development of Argentina's contemporary theatrical maturity.

Jewish dramatists in Argentina entered the mainstream in Spanish in two ways. First, there was the attempt to represent eloquently Jewish culture in the midst of indifference and aggressive anti-Semitism. Second, they undertook to comment critically on the dominant culture from the perspective of one of its major, often ignored, immigrant components. In an important sense, Jewish dramatists in Argentina are, beginning in the 1930s, accomplished spokesmen for their own culture and its concerns in the relative isolation of the Southern Hemisphere. Moreover, they especially exemplify the general issue of the marginalization of those ethnic and social subcultures that fall outside the scope of the dominant, nationalistic, and official one. Argentine Jews have pursued various strategies of assimilation into the dominant Hispanic and Catholic culture in Argentina, including virtually the complete abandonment of any distinctive Jewish identity, and one of the concerns of works by Jewish writers has been the problem of identity, assimilation, and relations with the dominant culture.

Several principles define the scope of this study. In the first place, no significant contribution to the analysis of cultural texts can be made by merely surveying a large inventory of works with brief comments on "themes and techniques." As a consequence, only a handful of prominent examples are analyzed here in the belief that an understanding of how a particular range of sociocultural issues are inscribed in theatrical texts is possible only if those texts are examined in considerable detail. Schallman's study provides the sort of inventory this chapter does not. Concomitantly, there would be little value in attempting to determine Jewish concerns by implication in works by Jewish authors that do not deal overtly with cultural experiences. Prominent Argentine dramatists whose roots are in the Jewish community—Osvaldo Dragún, Ricardo Halac, Diana Raznovich—have not, to the best of my knowledge, dealt with specifically ethnic matters, and there is no point in seeking an oblique Jewish consciousness or world view in their works.

The works that are examined are viewed as equally cultural texts and theatrical works. They are treated as artistic compositions that conform to structural principles that the critic may identify and assess; at the same time, it is recognized that whether read as a literary work or viewed as a theatrical performance, they involve meanings that are culturally, socially, and politically conditioned. Contemporary cultural criticism recognizes that artistic works must be examined both as special instances of meaning (their special artistic status, which we prize in our society) and as acts of communication whose signifying processes depend on correlations, no matter how complex these may be, with larger sociocultural meanings. It is in this sense that the following analyses are neither exclusively thematic (extrinsic) nor exclusively structural (intrinsic). Rather, this study accepts Lindstrom's premise in "Problems and Possibilities" that "by bringing to bear upon Jewish-Argentine writings the principled critical analysis of communicational and signifying process, this field of study will be able to illuminate what is most literary in the texts under examination" (125).

Eichelbaum's *Nadie la conoció nunca*, which has been virtually ignored by a theater criticism (Karavellos; Cruz) more interested in his dramas on rural themes or on psychological relationships, concerns Ivonne, an elegant and expensive courtesan who has lived for several years with Ricardito Iturbide (both the diminutive of his first name and the aristocracy of his surname reveal immediately that he is a very polished man about town). During the first act of the play, the casual conversation of assembled partygoers, who sip champagne in Ricardito's fancy apartment and with their witticisms vie for attention, touches on a number of inconsequential topics typical of such gatherings: the drinking habits of the guests, their extravagant tastes and other characteristics traits, the clichés of the day. They kid one of the guests about his musical talents, and he plays some tangos and other popular pieces, to which the guests dance. During the first half of the first act, Eichelbaum thus creates a theatrical space of easy and frivolous movement among an undifferentiated cast of characters. However, as the evening advances and the champagne flows ever more freely, the men begin to talk about what for them are harmless amusements, minor incidents marked by socially unacceptable behavior that can be readily dismissed as the high spirits of men from good families just having fun, even if it is at the expense of the less advantaged.

The second half of the first act turns on the farcical reenactment by the guests of one such escapade involving several individuals present at Ricardito's party. A group of them encountered a venerable Jewish gentleman, dressed in traditional Orthodox garb and hurrying along the street, fearful of attracting attention. The temptation was too great for these gay blades, and they confronted him. A guest nicknamed Obispo ("bishop," because of the color of the shirts he fancies) and an Anglo-Argentine named John undertake to re-create this enlightening dramatic situation:

JOHN.—Eso es, histórico. El cuento no es tan gracioso para ser contado; pero ha sido una cosa irresistible para quien lo ha visto. El ruso lo miraba con un terror verdaderamente cómico. Y Carlitos, muy serio, con esa seriedad de mamao fúnebre que tenía por esos días, le preguntaba: "¿Vos sos argentino?" Ahora van a ver. Yo soy el ruso, che. (A todos.) Ahora van a

ver qué cosas macanudas. (*A El Obispo.*) Vos hacés de Carlitos. (*John, como si fuera un intérprete de raza, con verdadero
celo artístico, busca todas las prendas necesarias para carac-
terizar al ruso. Se hunde una galera hasta cubrirse las orejas, se
pone un sobretodo a guisa de saco y con una servilleta simula
una barba.*) (49)[1]

If the first act of the play centers on the "public" livingroom of
the apartment and stresses the frivolous and extrovert antics of a
gallery of drunken guests, the second act centers on the intimate
refuge of Ricardito's and Ivonne's bedroom. The act begins with
Ivonne entering the room from the theatrical space of the previous
act. Gripped by intense and agitated emotion, she flings herself into
a chaise lounge as Ricardito enters to demand an explanation for
her reaction to John's story and for slapping another partygoer. We
understand full well that the relationship between the two entitles
him to such an explanation, and Ivonne consequently has no reservations about meeting his angry reproach with a forthright answer.

The response provided by Ivonne is the secret story of her life,
which she has never revealed to Ricardito. As the party continues in
the other room—a deft theatrical strategy to remind the audience of
the reality on which the relationship between Ricardito and Ivonne
has hitherto been based—in the refuge of her boudoir, dominated
by the luxurious bed that is the reminder of their involvement with
each other, Ivonne explains that she is a Jew, that she became sepa-
rated from her family during a pogrom in her native Poland (women
of easy virtue in Argentina at the time were often reputed to be
Polish Jews, and *polaca* was often understood to mean whore). She
entered a life of prostitution because it was all that was open to a
girl of her background (there are many treatments of the pathetic
if fascinating story of Jewish prostitution in Argentina. The most
recent, and certainly the best documented, is Bristow, chap. 4; also
Glickman). Ivonne goes on to tell that she learned by accident that
her father had ended up in Argentina also, but that, when she tried
to find him, she discovered that he had been killed in the anti-Semitic
violence in Buenos Aires during the Tragic Week of January 1919

(the Semana Trágica was the worst outbreak of persecution against Jews in Latin America since the Inquisition [Viñas; Weisbrot 200–201; Senkman 101–3]). It is for these reasons that Ivonne, breaking her silence about her own Jewish roots, roots that she feels she has abjured by nonobservance of the law and by leading an unclean life, was unable to contain herself any longer as a spectator to the charade put on by Ricardito's friends.

The dramatic revelations of the first half of the second act are in antiphonic relationship to the frivolity of the first half of the first act. And even more so, the happy dénouement of the second half of the second act is a response to the sudden emotional outburst that characterizes the end of the first act. After tense moments of confrontation and accusation, the two lovers find that Ivonne's revelation has served not to drive them irremediably apart but to cement their commitment. Their words of reconciliation embody the liberal tenet that the melding of opposites produces cultural and racial harmony (61–62). This happy ending underscores Eichelbaum's belief in a binding social contract whereby the full revelation of a society's secrets will promote the healing of a festering wound. What is particularly noteworthy about Eichelbaum's drama is the excellent sense of theatricality it displays. This is evident in the balanced rhythm of the two parts of the two acts and the use of the physical space of the two acts for an interplay between superficial and profound meanings for the relationship of the two main characters. This theatricality involves an ironic stance toward the audience and the latter's legitimate quest for satisfactory meaning in a cultural text. The frivolous behavior and aimless conversation of the group of bon vivants and their courtesans throughout the first act are a parody of a form of irreflexive and mindless social behavior that is echoed in the stupid farce the drunken men reenact for the amusement of the bored women.

The challenge to the audience is not to accept the representation of Ricardito's party (and the subsequent representation within a representation) as a grotesque parody of the life-style of a stratum of Argentine society. The markers framing this representation as sarcastic parody are too obvious to require belaboring: the decor, the dress, the manners, the topics of conversation, the witless nature of the interpersonal relationships of the characters are all stereotypes that would be nothing more than caricatures if it weren't for the "corrective" dénouement of the first act, which brings the play back to the realm of the interplay of serious ideas characteristic of the sort of thesis drama of the day *Nadie la conoció nunca* exemplifies.

The challenge to the audience of the play is based on the degree to which the parody of a social class can be used to underscore a significant interpretation of a sociocultural hypothesis. In the case of Eichelbaum's drama, that hypothesis involves the premise that people like Ivonne possess a hidden personal story that, in the horror of its tragic dimensions, can never be assimilated to the thoughtless life style-of those like Ricardito and his friends. Furthermore, the underlying hypothesis of the play implies the assumption that the revelation of a story such as Ivonne's can lead to a salutary self-contemplation on the part of someone like Ricardito. The happy ending of the play (which may or may not appear schematic in terms of the modern preference for more ambiguous, inconclusive, or open endings) is only possible because a new accord has been achieved between the two radically divergent life stories represented by Ricardito and Ivonne at the end of the first act.

The task assigned to the spectator, in terms of a theatrical competence that can derive meaning from the disparate assembly of often contradictory elements, is to appreciate how the apparent inconsequentialities of the first act are given meaning by Ivonne's revelations in the second act. The fact that it is difficult for the spectator to attach any significance to the behavior of the characters during the first act, other than as the antics of a group of bored—and boring—partygoers is what lends eloquence to Ivonne's explanation of her outrage over John's farce and the slap she gives the party guest. The slap both breaks the mood of the party and signals the transition from the first to the second act, from its texture as parody to its nature as a vehicle for sociocultural commentary. Ricardito's words opening the second act are spoken as an angry and aggressive demand for an explanation addressed to a mistress who has deviated from the role assigned to her. In this context, they take on a special resonance as the demand for sociocultural explanation at the heart of Eichelbaum's play.

The immediate goal of the Teatro Independiente movement in Argentina was the creation of a national professional theater. Such a theater, of which Samuel Eichelbaum was an important member, was primarily sensitive to and responsible for Argentine cultural needs during a period of considerable social and political crisis. Foreign models were to be drawn upon only insofar as they helped to satisfy these needs. As I have shown elsewhere (*Argentine Teatro Independiente*), this movement was an outstanding success in providing the bases for the impressive accomplishments of contemporary Argentine drama.

As was often the case with many of the innovative cultural movements in Argentina in the twentieth century, the major voices were often not of traditional Creole stock, and immigrant family names abound: Leónidas Barletta (Italian), Roberto Arlt (German), Conrado Nalé Roxlo (Catalan), Israel Zeitlin (who wrote under the name of César Tiempo) and Samuel Eichelbaum (Jewish)—these are only a few of the obvious examples of this fact of Argentine cultural history. It is instructive to examine the range of immigrant names that predominate in Perla Zayas de Lima's *Diccionario de autores teatrales argentinos*. When certain critics questioned the balance of national commitment versus international influences discernible in the works of these writers, alleging to find on occasion a greater apparent commitment to the direct translation of foreign modes, it was not surprising that these dramatists felt that their national loyalties were being challenged. This was particularly true given the fact that the period in question often reveals alarming ethnic prejudices against the children of immigrants and the non-Hispanic (*pace* Catalan) languages and customs.

Toward the end of his life, Eichelbaum felt it necessary to react against these judgments spanning the fifty years of his theatrical activity. After summarizing the influences that were often gratuitously or superficially attributed to this or that work, he continues:

> Pero si por estas razones las influencias subrayadas no podían disminuirme, la acusación de extranjerizante, para un escritor que se llama como me llamo, presuponía una posición espiritual, y acaso mental, también, en oposición a la de un

vasto sector de pueblo solidarizado con la hermosa empresa
de crear un teatro nacional, del que yo aspiraba, desde la más
incipiente adolescencia—en sueño y vigilia constantes—ser
un buen albañil. Era natural entonces que rechazara, íntima y
profundamente, tan arbitraria imputación.

Para demostrar este grueso error, no habrán de valerme
palabras sino hechos, y muy claros. Me fue preciso apelar
a un mundo de cosas subyacentes en la intimidad, desde los
años iniciales de mi vida, en la primera etapa de la formación
espiritual, en la que alternaron, por venturosa casualidad,
campo y ciudad argentinos, conjugados en una intrépida
infancia. ("Prólogo," in *El judío Aaron* 2–3)[2]

Eichelbaum proceeds to enumerate those plays of his in which he
deals with Argentine themes from his childhood. Some of these
themes involve the traditional creole motifs of the gauchos (*Un tal
Severando Gómez* [Someone Named Severando Gómez; 1942]) or
the *compadritos* (political bosses and party hacks; *Un guapo de 900*
[A 1900 Dandy; 1940]), the latter perhaps his most famous play (see
Foster, *Argentine Teatro Independiente,* chap. 3). Some of the works
involve that most crucial of all Argentine sociocultural motifs, the
immigrant communities. In this case, it is a question of the rural
Jewish settlements in the province of Entre Ríos from which sprang
so many important Argentine writers, Eichelbaum among them. The
theme of *El judío Aaron* (Aaron the Jew) is discussed briefly by Leonardo Senkman: "Eichelbaum intentó hacer la crítica del sistema
de explotación capitalista sobre el cual estaba basado el regimen de
trabajo agrícola en las colonias judías" (64).[3]

Set in Entre Ríos in 1925 (it was first performed in 1926), *El judío
Aarón* centers on the second generation of Jewish settlers, either
those settlers who arrived to reap the benefits of the first waves of
immigrants or the children of the latter, who may still have pre-
served a deep commitment to a traditional Jewish way of life but
who nevertheless felt themselves to be Argentines (cf. Aínsa). The
two young people of the play are just such thoroughly Argentine
citizens, as their names indicate. Goyito and Cecilia, unable to cope

with the bickering conflict between their immigrant fathers, elope to Buenos Aires, leaving Cecilia's father to rage over her rebelliousness and Goyito's father to praise his son's spirited initiative. But the play does not directly concern the decision of the two youths. Their love for each other and their decision to flee to the big city in order to make an independent life away from the conflict are only dramatic actions that underscore the basic point of contention of the play.

Like all of Eichelbaum's theater, *El judío Aarón* deals with sociocultural values and with both the tragic and comic effects of the blind adherence to beliefs that are accepted irreflexively with little regard for their inherent contradictions or their inappropriateness to an individual. In the case of *El judío Aarón*, Cecilia's father, Kohen, has accepted, with no apparent qualms, the profit economy of agrarian Argentina. Although he continues to speak with the heavy accent and the fragmented syntax of an untutored immigrant, Kohen endorses enthusiastically the principles of economic exploitation more articulately defended by the creole landowners or the well-educated Jews (e.g., Roter, the secretary of the farm cooperative, or Gorovich, the village doctor). The latter speak impeccable Spanish, whereas Kohen (and Efraín, the president of the farm cooperative) are virtual caricatures of the Jewish immigrant who can never master the language. These linguistic registers serve as important dramatic signs to characterize the position of the older immigrant relative to that of his children and the worldly members of the immigrant colony. Aarón, Goyito's father, also speaks with a thick Yiddish accent. But his social and economic values are diametrically opposed to those of Kohen and his supporters. Aarón champions a position that we can roughly associate with the old socialist Bund movement. His goal is for the cooperative to be truly a cooperative, a *fondo comunal*, in which monetary transactions are replaced by an exchange of goods; as a consequence, the profit motive would be eliminated. Supported by the rural *tapes* (mestizo peasants) but vociferously opposed by Kohen, Gorovich, the other landowners and the non-Jewish representatives of political power and the prevailing economic system who consider the idea of a cooperative highly dangerous, Aarón is alone in denouncing economic exploitation (Zago provides a fine pictorial representation of these communities). Aaron accuses Kohen, his principal adversary, of having sold out to the Argentine capitalist system. By contrast, Aarón prides himself on representing the ancient Jewish values of a communal and nonexploitative society. Significantly, his antagonists are incapable of grasping his utopian proposal, and, in one of their first exchanges (8), the distance between their two societal visions is marked by the interplay of native versus immigrant Spanish in the exchange between the two Jewish colonists (8).

Needless to say, everyone feels that Aarón's project is the delusion of a madman or the design of a dangerous anarchist (always the bogeyman of early twentieth-century Argentine political conflict), if not both. Through various scenes, we see Aarón in conflict with the Comisario, a heavy-handed caricature of arbitrarily exercised local creole authority, with his fellow immigrant landowners, with his own son, with some of the non-Jewish peasants, supported only by his creole housekeeper, Tomasa, and the *tapes,* who are exploited by the Kohens and the Goroviches of the village. In a nice comic touch, Tomasa (who identifies with Aarón to the extent of adopting some Yiddish words and phrases, surely a gesture of secret love!) insists that Aarón is, despite the calumnies against him, a "good Christian," whereas his opponents are simply "bad Christians."

When Goyito, unable to overcome Aarón's opposition to having him as a son-in-law, whisks Cecilia away to Buenos Aires, Aarón is elated. In his monomaniacal view of things, he sees his son's assertion of love for Cecilia as the triumph of his own point of view (19). It is significant that the only Yiddish phrase of the entire play—the time-honored lament of despair Veh ist mir! (Woe unto me)—is uttered by Kohen when he is informed that his daughter has eloped with Aarón's son. Yiddish is, of course, the language of their common traditional background (the Jewish settlers in Entre Ríos were exclusively East European), the very background that Aarón evokes in his utopian scheme of communal resources. This phrase mediates between the two linguistic registers that dominate the play until the final scene: the "good" Spanish of those Jews who have accepted and assimilated to the Argentine way of life and the fractured immigrant speech of an older generation that embodies the conflict of the transition from Old World values to the economic realities of Argentina. Kohen appears to have completed the transition, but Aarón refuses to. Aarón's triumph at the end of the play, which induces his antagonist to lapse in the language of the Old World that he has repudiated, is simply the vindication of a significant non-Argentine set of values. It is not necessary to belabor the ironic implication of this fact for Eichelbaum's refuge in the memories of his Argentine childhood as a response to the accusations of "foreignizing" in his theater.

All works of Argentine literature dealing with the experiences of the Jewish agricultural pioneers in Entre Ríos recall the idyllic narrative sketches of Alberto Gerchunoff's *Los gauchos judíos* (1910), a work that bespeaks the optimistic fervor of the first Argentine Centennial of the year of its publication (cf. Senkman, Primera Parte, cap. 2). There is, however, a more directly significant pre-text for *El judío Aarón* than Gerchunoff's rosy-hued portrait. I have in mind Florencio Sánchez's *La gringa* (The Dago Girl; 1904), surely the greatest classic of the Argentine stage. A pre-text is a chronologically previous work that although it may not have influenced the author in his composition, is recalled by the reader (or by the spectator, in the case of the theater) and provides resonances important for the understanding of the work being seen or read. It is not unusual for texts to stand in a relationship of contradiction or counterpoint to their pre-texts. This is essentially what is meant when we say that *Don Quixote* satirizes the books of chivalry or that Borges deconstructs major texts of Western metaphysics.

Sánchez's *La gringa* also involves a young couple whose marriage suggests the possible resolution of a cultural conflict among immigrants. However, in the case of Sánchez's play the woman is the daughter of an ambitious Italian immigrant (the title means "the Italian immigrant woman" in Argentine slang), and the man is the son of a gaucho who, although he may not be slothful, is certainly not motivated by the same drives to exploit the land as is the immigrant in his new-found land of opportunity. The drama is a very artful elaboration of the cultural conflict between the two fathers and their respective interpretations of the meaning of the Argentine soil (see the analysis of the dramatic structure of the play in Foster,

"Ideological Shift"). Thus the final union of the two children is the triumph of the imperative for gauchos and gringos—native Argentines and immigrants—to make their peace and live side-by-side in a modern Argentina. Sánchez's only optimistic play (the majority of his dramas follow the Ibsenian model of plays such as *Ghosts, The Wild Duck, An Enemy of the People,* and so forth), *La gringa* represents a social accord that was more an ideal than a reality at the time of its first performances, and the play clearly promotes the triumph of social accord through simple love. Eichelbaum leaves open to the spectator's individual interpretation whether the union of Goyito and Cecilia augurs a harmony (whatever its nature may be) between the antagonistic positions represented by Aarón and Kohen, or the possible triumph of Aarón's utopian social program, or whether it is merely Aarón's gleeful revenge against his ideological enemies. One can suspect the latter is the most interesting interpretation of the play's conclusion. But the important point is that the categorical resolution of social conflict at the heart of *La gringa* is absent from *El judío Aarón.* Clearly, Eichelbaum's probings in the memories of his childhood could not yield the image of rural immigrant social harmony Sánchez's classic example of cultural mythification could.

Nevertheless, the relationship between *El judío Aarón* and *La gringa* must be explored on a level far deeper than the simple disjunction between the respective resolutions, one pessimistic and the other optimistic, regarding immigrant colonization of the Argentine countryside. In *La gringa,* the social pact at issue concerns two groups, one, at least initially, external to the cultural ideology of the country (the Italians) and the other internal (the creoles). Although given the principles of immigration fostered by the *próceres* (worthies), the triumph of the former is understandable, *La gringa,* as a dramatic interpretation of reality, can only be called utopian in nature, because Sánchez had no way of knowing how, in fact, his *gringos* would prevail at the expense of creole culture—and, indeed, that creole culture would be rewritten in terms of the assimilation, and perhaps even the primacy, at least as far as Buenos Aires and the littoral are concerned, of Italian immigrant culture. Beginning with the figure of President Pellegrini, but especially with the long shadow cast by Juan Domingo Perón and the much-vaunted fact that a significant number of recent military dictators were of Italian origin (not to mention the whole *cocoliche/lunfardo* shtick—if one be allowed such a trope), the Italianization of Argentine metropolitan culture is very much of a done deed, and in ways Sánchez could not even have imagined.

By contrast, in the cast of Eichelbaum's play, the problematical social contract involves conflict within an outsider group, and, indeed, one treated as homogenous by the Hispanic creole/Italianized creole hegemonic culture, unable as it is to assay in any appreciable way the profound divisions that very early on arose within the Jewish immigrant community, whether urban or, as in the case of *El judío Aarón*, rural. (One might evoke here the role played by Gerchunoff's *Los gauchos judíos* [The Jewish Gauchos of the Pampas] in naturalizing quite another utopian view of immigrant culture, one contemporaneous with Sánchez's and just as leveling in its ideological effects.) The division within Eichelbaum's play—and, to be sure, one announced by the biographical reference to his own *intrépida infancia*—turns on the split between the conservation of a relocated Jewish traditional way of life and the imperative to achieve some level of sociocultural assimilation. Given names are certainly the semiotic markers of this division, and names in turn bespeak larger linguistic considerations. Whereas in the case of the Italian immigrants, both to the extent that Italian is basically a cognate language with Spanish (even when assessed in terms of the many dialects represented by an abstract "Italian") and given names in Italian easily migrate over into their Spanish equivalents, the Jewish immigrants not only represented a multiplicity of often mutually unintelligible languages (and even widely diverse dialects of the presumably common heritage of Yiddish), but whatever linguistic medium was spoken by any one specific immigrant was virtually noncontinuous with Spanish. Thus Spanish for the Jewish immigrants was a foreign language in ways it could never be for the Italian immigrants, and Jewish/Hebrew names, even when part of a subsequently officially recognized permissible Judeo-Christian name, could never be anything but the alien Other: Samuel ("para un escritor que se llama como me llamo [yo]") inalterably marks a social space that lies on the far side of one of Argentina's great social divides.

The assumption of appropriately Hispanic names, the acquisition of a cultivated norm of Spanish quite superior to anything any economically successful Italian immigrant thought it necessary to perfect, are the essential markers for a Jewish identity that defines itself in terms of its ideological—and, therefore, its economic—approximation to a hegemonic social pact that leaves any bracketable Jewish identity in the possession of cantankerous and barely tolerated primitive elders. Aarón and Singer exemplify the disjunction being characterized here, but it is significant to note that *both* of their children, irrespective of their parents' beliefs, have acquired acceptable creole names: Cecilia and Goyito, respectively, and, of course, they both speak "good" Spanish, as does Singer. It is in this context that one can understand Eichelbaum's concern over his own name, Samuel, and the way in which it irreducibly marks his Jewishness. The imperative felt by the descendants of the Singers to submerge traditional Jewish cultural motifs in the dominant culture does much for our understanding of how one of the founders of the contemporary cosmopolitan theater in Argentina, despite having been raised, so to speak, in the same shetl as *el judío Aarón,* produced only one work dealing with the subject of Jewish-Argentine cultural conflict—in the 1960s, at the end of his major dramatic production, and, to be best of my knowledge, never performed. Moreover, the bulk of Eichelbaum's plays, despite a text such as *Un guapo de 900* and *Un tal Severando Gómez,* exemplify the criterion of urban plays of sophisticated manners and psychological profiles, cultural modalities that, precisely, bespeak the creole cultural hegemony toward which Singer looks and which Cecilia and Goyito, now quite unconsciousness and "naturally," exemplify, in a way that cannot help but confirm the increasingly impotent sociocultural paternity of those who are called Aarón and, of course, Samuel.

It would be difficult to overestimate the importance of César Tiempo (the pen name of Israel Zeitlin, 1906–80) in the development of the Teatro Independiente movement. This movement brought many creative strands of Argentine culture together in an energetic renovation of the theater. As has already been noted with reference to Eichelbaum, one aspect of the movement was the incorporation into the theater of Argentina's many immigrant groups, their concerns and their idioms. Of particular importance, along with the Italian element, was the emergence of a strong Jewish component, and no one typified this ethnic contribution more than César Tiempo. The thirties saw the transition from a flourishing Yiddish theater in Buenos Aires to the participation of Jewish actors, directors, dramatists, and other theater people in the national theater in Spanish, a transition reflective of the increasingly greater participation of Jews in Argentina's cultural and social life during the period (to understand the validity of this statement, one need only examine the names of individuals in these categories listed in the documentary sections of Marial; see also Weisbrot 175–208). Tiempo's major work is, without a doubt, *Pan criollo* (Native Bread), which won the Premio Nacional de Teatro in 1937, the first work by a Jewish dramatist to earn this honor. *Pan criollo* is symptomatic of the desire of certain representatives in the Jewish community in Argentina to downplay their otherness in a society that was going through an intensely nationalistic phase with alarming fascist overtones (soldiers had goosestepped to the Presidential Palace when the military staged the country's first military coup on 6 September 1930). The play also reflects the concern for writers and artists to espouse eloquently their ethnic and minority identity for purposes of informing the Catholic, creole Argentines that remained in firm control of the private and official mechanisms of culture in the country. Several of Tiempo's works fulfill this goal, but *Pan criollo* remains his most memorable effort. I have written elsewhere about the nature of this drama:

> *Pan criollo* is . . . an intensively patriotic play, and there are only vague traces of the problems surrounding the place of nonintegrationist Jews in Argentine society. Perhaps no other work of Argentine literature, with the possible exception of Alberto Gerchunoff's *Los gauchos judíos* (1910) about the rural Jewish settlements in the province of Entre Ríos, paints such a positive image of the possibility of Jews and non-Jews living side by side in Argentina and contributing to the realization of national myths of the Liberal society. These myths

had served as the sociocultural norms of Argentine society until the military coup of 1930, and many Argentines were convinced that they continued to constitute a valid national program to which the country would in time return . . .

Pan criollo concerns the conflict between Don Salomón and his daughter Lía, a high-strung young woman who has fallen in love with her father's gentile secretary. After a stormy confrontation between father and daughter, on the occasion of matchmaker's bringing to meet the family a decidedly unappealing candidate for Lía's hand, Lía and the secretary run away. Don Salomón, crushed at this sign of his incompetence in maintaining patriarchal authority and incensed over his daughter's violation of Jewish custom, considers her dead. In his humiliation, he resigns his judicature and moves his family to the country to begin a new life. However, between these two decisions, Jehovah appears to him to warn him to be more understanding toward Lía and to promise him that she will return to reclaim her place in the family. Lía does in fact return. Her lover asks that the father accept him on the grounds that his sincere love for Lía is more important than the fact that he is a gentile. Meanwhile, Don Salomón's neighbors insist that he become their new mayor by virtue of his exemplary representation of both Jewish culture and Argentine nationalism. On this happy note, the play ends. (*Argentine Teatro Independiente* 111–12)

Because I have examined *Pan criollo* in detail, with particular emphasis on the theatrical use of cultural concepts, I will not repeat my observations here. Suffice it to say that in view of subsequent Argentine sociopolitical history, the play has a decidedly quaint and Pollyannaish ring to it; the thrust of Senkman's comments are a bit more severe, as signaled by the title of his section on the play: "La integración judeo-argentina a pesar del antisemitismo" (176–89). Nevertheless, *Pan criollo* remains a landmark example of the theatrical articulation on a national scale of a specifically Jewish motif.

Prior to the notable success of *Pan criollo,* Tiempo had already staged works dealing with the Jewish presence in Argentina. Of particular note is an example of Pirandellian theater, *El teatro soy yo; farsa dramática en tres actos* (I'm the Theater; a Farce in Three Acts; 1933), Tiempo's first dramatic work. Metatheatrical in its utilization of one theatrical work to frame a second one that impinges on and interprets the former, *Teatro* is also Pirandellian in its manipulation of the convention that equates life and the drama.

Tiempo's play, seen from the perspective of thirty years, is, quite frankly, a strange work. The essentially enthusiastic notices it received, from both the Jewish and general Argentine press when it opened on 3 November 1933 at the Teatro Smart (under the direction of Enrique Gustavino and performed by the Compañía de Teatro Moderno), touch only tangentially on the plot and its elaborations (see the extensive appendix of reviews in the published edition of the play [181–219]).

Teatro is the story of the strained relationship between two playwrights, Myriam Sambatión and Gaspar Liberión; she is Jewish, he is black. During the rehearsal of one of Sambatión's works (she has numerous successes to her credit), Liberión arrives for a rehearsal of his first play, which is to be produced by the same director as Sambatión's. Pinch-hitting for an absent actress in Liberión's play, Sambatión interrupts the rehearsal to accuse the former of having plagiarized his text from Oscar Wilde. As a consequence, the director expels Liberión from the theater; a newspaper reporter who has happened by to write a story on Sambatión's new success publishes an article on Liberión's purported theatrical fraud.

After a confrontation between the two playwrights that turns on the parallels in their lives resulting from discrimination, Sambatión, now convinced that Liberión's play does not really involve plagiarism after all, agrees to assist Liberión in having the play produced. However, renewed conflict between them arises when Sambatión angrily rejects Liberión's amorous advances; it is clear that the rebuff has racial overtones. The Jewish dramatist, nevertheless, makes good her promise to assist Liberión in producing his play, and it is a thunderous success. But when the black dramatist joins the cast in a curtain call to acknowledge applause, he is the victim of a racial slur from a member of the audience. He thereupon shoots himself, and, as he lies dying, he ignores Sambatión's tearful protestations of love and asserts that he has failed to transcend his human condition. In the face of social prejudice, he and not his work is the theatrical event to which the public responds, and not even God is able to alter the script that demands Liberión's humiliation and death. Hence, the title of the play.

What is peculiar about Tiempo's play is not so much the insistence with which it correlates racial discrimination against blacks in Argentina with discrimination against Jews. Several of the original review notices underscore this rhetorical equivalence, and Leonardo Senkman has evaluated these responses as evidence of Argentina's national self-satisfaction (more on this below: "La integración posible del judío argentino durante la Década Infame" [172–76]). Suffice it to note that at the time of *Teatro,* Jews were playing an increasing role in the nation's cultural life while experiencing various degrees of open and covert discrimination that ranged from the annoying to the humiliating. Blacks, on the other hand, had all but disappeared from all levels of Argentine society, and it was still a decade before anti-Perónists would revitalize the racial slurs against blacks by applying them to the massive migration into Buenos Aires of provincials, many with Indian roots, that Perón's policies encouraged.

Rather, what most seems strange about Tiempo's play is his having cast it as a farce, an essentially comic theatrical subgenre. Indeed, the majority of the characters in the play and the dramatic situations involve various forms of stereotyping typical of the farce. If the two playwrights identify themselves with traits associated with their backgrounds—or at least have such traits repeatedly attributed to them—the supporting characters rarely rise above the level of stock farcical types: the newspaper reporter is a model of venality and professional sarcasm, traits that spare him the bother of seeing the theatrical works he reviews; Sambatión's mother is an anthology of the gestures and mannerisms of a vulgar yenta; the actors barely bother with the roles they must play; and the director, the producer, and the stagehands give credence to the worst that can be said about their professions. Only the Actor de Carácter, the leading man whom we first see rehearsing Sambatión's play and then starring in Liberión's success, shows any signs of differentiated behavior. It is he who serves as a bridge between the Jew and the black, working to overcome the distrust and hard feelings between the two by evoking a code of human understanding that the final dénouement clearly belies.

The figures of the Jew and the black are a productive compromise between the stereotype and unique human characters. If Sambatión is defined as the aggressive Jew who triumphs by the sheer energy of her will and the force of her creative efforts, we are shown her vulnerability in the face of memories of her social background as the daughter of immigrants and her realization that she has the ethical responsibility to temper her personal drive with a comprehension of the misfortunes of others. Her denunciation of Liberión throughout the play is transformed from the resounding putdown of a professional rival into an understanding of his sufferings at the hands of racial discrimination, and her own racially motivated rejection of his amorous advances is replaced by her tender feelings toward him at the end of the play. Liberión, who is the more complex of the two, must define his ambitions as deriving from a drive to understand human suffering rather than only from a desire for personal triumph over racial prejudices. Sambatión's promise to assist him in producing his play—a gesture that marks her transition from caricature to differentiated human character—is based on her comprehension of the depth of Liberión's character. And the violent final scene, in which Liberión realizes that the success of his play is meaningless in the face of the human drama in which he is the central figure, confers upon him an ultimate, if belated, tragic dimension.

This movement from farce to tragedy is what is most peculiar about Tiempo's play, and one that the criticism has not underscored sufficiently. Farce is an important ingredient of the Teatro Independiente movement, and it foreshadows and eventually merges with the more sophisticated nonnaturalistic, antipsychological devices of Brechtian theater in the 1960s, particularly the mode that has been called the *grotesque* (Blanco Amores de Pagella 17–27; Neglia, *Aspectos* 5–14). The important ingredient in farce is the stereotype: a character meant to display one or two clearly identifiable human traits. Because the nuances of motivation and the complexity of human relations are not features of the farce, dramatic texture is based primarily on the ingeniousness of dramatic situations and their various combinations. In the case of *Teatro,* this is accomplished by both the play's Pirandellian framework and metatheatrical element.

Tiempo's play is metatheatrical in the sense that it deals with the business of theater. Two plays are the motivating force of dramatic action: Sambatión's play on a Jewish theme (based on the story in Jeremiah 13 about the linen girdle) and the disastrous rehearsal but subsequent successful production of Liberión's play (its theme is not revealed to viewers of *Teatro*). Both plays are used to define the basic conflict of *Teatro* as embodied in the actors and the theater people engaged in producing Sambatión's and Liberión's plays. The Jewish-inspired text deals with how something of value is of little use and rots if allowed to remain hidden: for Liberión, Sambatión's play attests to how her drive for success has stifled her feelings for her Jewish heritage and its ethical commitment to suffering mankind. Liberión feels particularly ill-treated by her because her insensitivity and cruelty belie her own cultural origins and her personal story as the victim of social misunderstanding and prejudice:

> MYRIAM.—[. . . S]e ensañaban con mi condición de judía.
> GASPAR.—Eso debió haberla enorgullecido. Y sobre todo
> hacer que comprendiese mi situación. Somos nosotros, en
> realidad, los modernos judíos. Llevamos en la piel, tiznada
> para siempre, como una marca infamante, el signo de la raza.
> Ustedes se confunden, se mezclan, se disgregan, truecan sus
> apellidos y hasta su religión. Y el mundo los acepta y hasta los
> recibe con esa alegría con que se obtiene una presa valiosa.
> (121–22)[4]

Because its theme is not so clearly known to the audience, the meta-theatrical nature of Liberión's work cannot be as easily identified as can that of Sambatión's play, *El cinto de lino* (The Linen Sash). *La ciudad silenciosa* (The Silent City), however, is a success, and it is the success of his play that turns against Liberión. The people around him cannot understand why he ignores the audience's cries of "author!" Liberión concludes that his play is a false success because of the hard feelings that continue to exist between him and Sambatión. When she sends him a sarcastic note on opening night, his feelings are even more hurt, and he is plunged into even deeper despair. And when the actors drag him on stage at the end of the play and he is the object of the racial slur that causes him to shoot himself, the repudiation of his success is categorical. In this oblique sense, the success of *La ciudad silenciosa* bespeaks the failure of Liberión's attempts at resolving his personal conflict.

The Pirandellian element of the play, of course, consists of the homology between life and drama. But where Pirandello is credited with the belief that theater is not the representation of real life but that real life is earnest theatricality, Liberión's assertion that he is the central figure in a play that not even God can rewrite is more of a rhetorical conceit to underscore the tragic sense of his situation as exemplary victim of racial discrimination, hatred, and misunderstanding. Liberión's interpretation, although important for signaling the transition from farce to tragedy in Tiempo's play, does not, in my opinion, really expand the artistic potential of Pirandello's hypothesis. Clearly, the situation of Jews and blacks in Western society in the 1930s was not a matter of the staged conventions of life but of serious social dynamics beyond the control of the "characters of the drama," a circumstance that refutes implicitly the Pirandellian corollary that human beings are the playwrights of their own theatrical existence, or are at least active forces in it (the Pirandellian influence in the play is discussed by Neglia, *Pirandello* 107–11). Of greater interest, instead, is the perception that the nature of the theatrical enterprise, which for Sambatión is a successful translation of her personal ethnic experiences and for Liberión a false mask for a situation that cannot be remedied, is equally the victim of social stigma because of its unsettling treatment of the human condition.

Criticism on *Teatro* has appropriately questioned Tiempo's manner of highlighting the problem of discrimination, particularly felt by the Jews in the 1930s during the rise of nazism and the emergence in Argentina of military governments sympathetic to fascism (Navarro Gerassi), and Senkman has detailed this sociopolitical context of the play in detail. It is indeed curious that anti-Semitic sentiment in Argentina is highlighted by reference to antiblack feelings. Argentina, of course, is no less racially discriminatory, on the level of popular sentiment, than other Western societies: as the reaction to Perón's policy, a bit over a decade after *Teatro*, of encouraging the migration into Buenos Aires of workers from the northern provinces demonstrated with such pathetic eloquence. These workers, many of indigenous stock, were dismissed by the Porteños as *cabecitas negras*. But the simple fact is that Tiempo chose to have his play hinge on the figure of a social type that, although it corresponded to abiding feelings of racial discrimination, did not, in sociological fact, constitute an authentic presence in Argentine society at the time of the play: there were hardly any blacks left in Argentina by the time in which the play is set. For some critics, such a fact invalidates the "realism" of the play. However, it is precisely in this sense that Tiempo's definition of his play as a *farsa* is of importance. The full subtitle of *Teatro* is *Farsa dramática indirecta o lo que a Ud. le parezca, en tres actos* (Indirect Dramatic Farse or Whatever You Think It Is, in Three Acts). The two operational phrases here are *indirecta* and *lo que a Ud. le parezca* (the latter reminiscent of Pirandello's 1917 *So It Is [If You Think So]*). Clearly, Tiempo's dramatic decision was to forego a dramatically naturalistic representation—say in the vein of Ibsen or Florencio Sánchez—for the possibilities of an "indirect" farce. The indirectness involves embodying the problems of social discrimination in a black character who is physically blocked from masking his status behind the changes of social identity Liberión accuses Jews of being attracted to, despite the biblical lesson of the linen girdle. There can be no doubt that Tiempo's play focuses on issues of Jewish identity in Argentina, and one presumes that the lesson of Sambatión's own play, as expounded to her by the tragic case of Liberión, will make her a more honest exponent of her own ethnic and religious culture. Viewed in this fashion, the strategy of rhetorical exaggeration in Tiempo's play, in the form of the Liberión stereotype and figure, confirms its quality as farce, but as farce in the service of serious social commentary.

Generational conflict is one of the enduring themes of universal literature: the rebellion of children against the allegedly outmoded moral and social criteria of their parents and the despair of the latter over that rebellion. Such a conflict assumes added dimensions in immigrant societies or subcultures, in which the misunderstandings between parents and children is aggravated by the often unconscious or unperceived alienation imposed on the rigors of coming of age by the cultural dislocations immigrants inevitably experience. As a consequence, if parents witnessing the loss of ethnic identity in their children awaken our pity for disappearing ways of life, there is truly a tragic dimension to the choices that those children are called upon to make.

Argentina, like the United States, is essentially an immigrant nation, and during the past one hundred years, groups of foreign-born citizens, such as Jews and Italians, to name only the most dominant groups, have been able to identify readily with works that describe the generational conflicts exacerbated by being cast in terms of a conflict of cultures. And just as in American literature, Argentine literature presents an abundance of works that express comic, pathetic, and tragic perspectives on this complex range of conflicts between foreign-born parents and their native children (cf. García; Sánchez Sívori).

Rozenmacher authored a number of works dealing with the cultural conflicts of Argentine Jews. He placed a special emphasis on the problem of the children of immigrants in maintaining their identity in an essentially hostile Latin American environment and in coming to terms with the traditional demands of their parents (cf. Sosnowski, "Germán Rozenmacher"). *Réquiem para un viernes a la noche* (Requiem for a Friday Night) is his most famous work dealing with the subject, and it is, of all of the works examined in this study, the one that most assumes a tragic dimension in its vision of the child of immigrants caught in crosscurrents of antagonist cultural forces.

Originally performed in 1964 by the IFT (Idisches Volks Theater)—one of the most distinguished of Argentina's Teatro Independiente companies—*Réquiem* is a deeply moving play about the break between the Argentine-born David and his cantor father, Sholem, now in decline.[5] Sholem is unable to accept his son's departures from custom and ritual, which he attempts at great emotional cost to maintain in the alien Argentine urban setting. David feels that he cannot make for himself an acceptable personal destiny circumscribed by oppressive tradition. In the final scene between the two, the father attempts to dress his son in the symbols of religion while speaking to him of his future as a cantor, insisting that David adhere to the identity of his forefathers. But David—for whom artistic expression means not the profession of cantor, or even vaudeville actor like his uncle Max, but writing literature, an occupation his father deprecatingly dismisses as a "hobby"—violently repudiates his father's gestures:

> DAVID.—(*Se desprende con violencia las vestiduras y las arroja, llorando.*) ¡Basta, papá!
> SHOLEM.—(*Se queda inmóvil, destrozado, no sabe qué hacer, balbucea, ya completamente derrotado, humillado.*) ¡David! Te estoy pidiendo por favor que te quedes.
> DAVID.—Me ahogo, papá, me asfixio, me estoy muriendo aquí dentro.
> SHOLEM.—David, pero me estás matando, estás aniquilando esta casa. ¿No te das cuenta? (*Comienza a ponerse de nuevo terrible y duro.*) ¿Te estás avergonzando de mí, de ser lo que sos? (45)[6]

It is shortly after this exchange that David leaves his father's house, and Sholem sits shiva for him, as if mourning the dead. The exchange between Sholem and David is virtually a cliché of the literature of generational conflict exacerbated by the misunderstandings between immigrant parents and their native-born children. Rather than from any thematic originality, Rozenmacher's play derives its dramatic impact from the carefully balanced portrayal of the moral and spiritual dilemma involved, from the contrapuntal juxtaposition of cultural codes in conflict, and from the suspension of the inevitable dénouement in order that the audience may weigh thoughtfully the essential points of conflict involved and their emotional consequences.

The most impressive theatrical device in *Réquiem* is the retardation of the appearance of David. Consisting of ten scenes (an opening "Réquiem" and nine numbered scenes) divided into the traditional three acts of Hispanic theater or the two acts that have become customary in contemporary staging, *Réquiem* is designed to run approximately as long as a play given single billing. David does not appear until the sixth scene, more than halfway through the play. In this way, the first scenes of the play turn on a character who is not physically present. He is referred to in various terms, his words and behavior are recalled, and his importance as a point of reference to the other characters—his parents, and his father's brother, who lives with the family in its modest apartment—is evoked.

The fact that David is an "absent presence" allows the other three characters to define him in terms of their own particular preoccupations, thereby providing a refracted definition of the conflict that centers on his concerns and frustrations. The father is obsessed, in almost a maniacal fashion, with observance. On the other hand, Max, although virtually an aging caricature of Argentina's equivalent of the vulgar and corny Borscht-Belt hoofer, defends his nephew with a more worldly understanding of the problems of maintaining traditional Jewish identity in a secular, Argentine society. Leie, David's mother, is alternately concerned to maintain her husband's authority and to minister as an indulgent mother to the preoccupations of her only son.

The scenes prior to the appearance of David, who arrives with the turbulence of self-centered youth, only to bring to the breaking point the tensions already developed during his absence, involve a series of permutations of the three senior characters. The three together, and in varying groups of two, comment on the issue at hand: How serious are David's gestures of independence from tradition? Max is convinced that too much is being made of them, and Leie pleads for indulgence for the weaknesses and excesses of the young. They also comment on the need to bring David's behavior into line with custom as they see it: Sholem is outraged at the ultimate insult that his son wishes to marry a woman named María, and Leie is determined to protect her ailing husband from the intemperate words of their son. Rozenmacher handles these scenes with consummate dramatic skill, making use of two principal theatrical strategies: details concerning deviation from accepted practices and the interplay of assertion and commentary.

The overall staging of *Réquiem* is meant to evoke a sense of decay and abandon, of loss and death. This sense is first the symbolic death of identity, as the characters comment on their struggle to maintain a sense of Jewishness in an alien and hostile country and on the centuries-old persecution of their people. Moreover, this sense foreshadows, of course, the figurative death of David, of the beloved son of the family, who brutally but tragically must sever the ties to a cultural tradition that he no longer feels is his. The dramatic texture of the play is an interplay between the signs of Jewish identity, from the Yiddish and Hebrew words used and the physical details of the staging to an entire outlook on life and experience, and references to the attempts to maintain that identity.

Throughout the play, there are admonitions, spoken essentially by Sholem, to respect the Sabbath, as well as denunciations of such-and-such an act or gesture or expression because it violates Sabbath law. For example, Leie's first speech moves quickly to a criticism of her brother-in-law for smoking in the house after the Friday sundown:

> ¿Usted qué hace ahí? Apague ese cigarrillo, ¡goy! ¡Ya estamos
> en viernes a la noche! No se puede fumar. Lo único que falta.
> . . Que entre Sholem y lo encuentre fumando. (11)[7]

At another point, when Max has confessed to discussing David's problems with him outside the house in a neighboring café, Leie also accuses him of acting just like a goy (22). For Sholem, his son's transgressions range from whistling in the house like the goyim cart drivers of his native Russian village (32) to dating a non-Jewish woman, and one whose name is María, on top of it (40).

Taken individually, these accusations are almost comically pathetic because of their emphasis on ritual law and tradition at the expense of the ethical sense at the heart of Judaism. But in *Réquiem* they are items in the accumulation of a sense of despair over what is a profoundly meaningful issue: the sense of an impending and irrevocable tragic loss of personal and collective identity. Two phrases reverberate in the dialogues of these older characters who have had to come to terms with a sociocultural reality that they have never come to accept as their own: Sholem's lament "No entiendo" (I don't understand; 23), "No entiendo, Max, ¡simplemente no entiendo!" (I don't understand, Max, I simply don't understand!; 32) and Leie's "Y todo eso está muerto" (And this is all dead now; 15). In this way, the insistent references to deviations from ritual aspects of law and custom assume the importance of signs that bespeak the larger issue of cultural tensions and spiritual and emotional dislocation that is the central dramatic conflict of the play. Senkman examines the play regarding the relationship David-María and the conflict Sholem-David (Senkman prefers the spelling Scholem [303–8]). Of special note are his observations about Sholem's "formal" Spanish, the reflex of his status as a cantor and his constant point of reference in the ritual language of Hebrew and his maternal Yiddish, and the natural colloquial Argentine Spanish of his son. This aspect is an important dramatic element for marking the distance between father and son.

The second strategy that characterizes those scenes of *Réquiem* that define the crisis of the Abramson family is the interplay between assertion and commentary. Assertion involves a statement by one of the characters—an opinion, an interpretation, a recollection. As a response to this assertion, one of the other characters provides a comment, which may take the form of a contradiction, a correction, or an elaboration. This pattern of dialogue interchanges functions on two levels. As a form of discordant phatic dialogue, it highlights the growing tensions that are destroying the Abramson household. As a give-and-take characterization of the concerns that ultimately revolve around the absent David, this pattern provides a cumulative statement of crisis and conflict. In one of the exchanges between Leie and Max, the strategy of assertion and commentary and the strategy of providing details of the sense of loss come together in an evocation of the contrast between Leie's home town and that of Max and Sholem (15).

As in the case of the comments concerning deviations from observance and folkways, the foregoing exchange, based on the boastful comparison of long-lost native villages, as an isolated bit of dialogue does not go beyond the recurring themes of nostalgic immigrant literature. But as Leie brings the conversation back to the still-absent David, who has promised his mother not to miss the Sabbath meal as a gesture of conciliation toward his father, it is apparent that Max's and Leie's idle banter is yet another detail for the characterization of the trauma the family is undergoing.

The pattern of assertion and commentary inevitably reaches its climax when David does arrive and when father and son, despite the efforts of the latter to avoid a confrontation, reach the conclusion that there is no choice but for David to leave Sholem's house and for the latter to consider him dead. The dialogue between the two concerning the traditional family occupation is an example of the use of the pattern of assertion and commentary as a device expressive of the central conflict of the play. And it serves to underscore the pathetic misunderstanding of father and son as their differences take them to the final breaking point. Sholem is incapable of backing away from the harsh judgment of his son's deviation from tradition; David cannot forego the outlook that comes from moving in the larger world of his native and non-Jewish Argentina, an attitude that seems to have become skewed toward favoring the non-Jewish. Weisbrot, in addressing the question of the secularization of the Argentine Jew, notes that "the striking detachment from Jewish identity is not at all exceptional among younger Argentine Jews; rather it reflects a widespread attempt to be 'pure Argentines'" (279).

Réquiem's most overt thrust may be with the rather specific problems of one aspect of generational conflict among Argentine Jews. It is obvious, however, that this problem has larger consequences as Rozenmacher formulates it. David Abramson's overriding concern, one that leads him to the heartrending step of breaking definitively with his family, with which he still has a deep emotional tie, is to decide the course of his own life outside a Jewishness that repulses him as both dull and confining. Such a choice may not inevitably involve what for Sholem are the scandalous steps of marrying a Gentile and renouncing Jewish observance. But the weighted rhetoric of the play leaves little doubt that Sholem foresees accurately the subsequent decisions David will make. The result is that the ideology of Rozenmacher's play and the source of its pathetic and ultimately tragic quality is the implicit rejection of a facile reconciliation between either Sholem's rigid views or David's New World rebellion. The sort of irresolvable generational and religiocultural conflict at the heart of *Réquiem* is not only meaningful for a Jewish Argentine audience, but it is one example of a theatrical text that provides a general, national public with an image of one significant element of its own overall social identity.

Although it is questionable whether those works that do not explicitly treat aspects of the Jewish experience within the framework of dominant Argentine culture are pertinent to this study, Rozenmacher's *El Lazarillo de Tormes* (1971) presents a special case. *Lazarillo* opened at the IFT on 7 May 1971, three months to the day before Rozenmacher's death in an automobile accident on 7 August.

Rozenmacher called his play a "versión teatral" of the anonymous early sixteenth-century picaresque prototype, and it is immediately clear that he accepts the prevailing interpretations of the picaresque as established by this narrative, specifically the role of the picaresque character as a figure both who embodies an explicit challenge to the official myths of Spain's glory during the so-called Golden Age of the 1600s and 1700s and who represents the cynical coming to terms with the circumstances of a decadent public life. Moreover, Rozenmacher sees in the Lazarillo figure an implicit revolutionary who, although in the end he accepts the conditions of survival in his society, nevertheless articulates through the narrative of his own life an unflinchingly sardonic evaluation of those conditions and the need to challenge them. The fact that although he may have cynically accepted the imperative to abide by the conditions of survival, Lazarillo is still able to represent those conditions ironically is one of the interesting narrative tensions of the original novel that Rozenmacher preserves in his theatrical version.

Rozenmacher preserves this irony in two ways. In the first place, in Brechtian terms reminiscent of the *Historias para ser contadas* (Stories for Telling) of Osvaldo Dragún, one of the most original dramatists in contemporary Argentina (Foster, "Estrategias narrativas"), Lazarillo is both the protagonist in the presentation of his picaresque life story and the narrator of that story who steps outside of it to address the audience. In the second place, Lazarillo addresses the audience as a self-conscious character and actor in a mid-twentieth century theatrical work. As a consequence, he speaks from the perspective of four hundred years of "experience" in being Lazarillo, thereby identifying Lazarillo's story with the recurring motifs of religious hypocrisy and social repression characteristic of Western society and the Hispanic legacy. He also speaks, particularly in the opening segment of the play, as an Argentine, with the vocabulary and verb forms that one usually associates with Buenos Aires middle-class speech. The relationship between Lazarillo's identity as a modern Argentine and the network of allusions of the picaresque anti-hero to a society in decline characterized by the oppression of the individual and an official, public hypocrisy hardly requires belaboring (it is important to recall that at the time of the play's opening, Argentina was in the middle of a series of repressive and self-serving military dictatorships).

The pivotal feature of this expansion of the meanings of the Lazarillo figure is Rozenmacher's one significant deviation from the sixteenth-century model (to which in other regards the play is so faithful that actual lines of the novel are quoted in the play). This deviation involves the introduction of the Inquisidor, the paradigmatic embodiment of the blind repression that was emerging as the dominant feature of Spanish culture during the late Renaissance, as a correlative of the collapse of that country's national and imperial structure and as one of Spain's abiding contributions to the constitution of Latin American society: "LAZARILLO.—Mi historia es que estoy vivo, y para siempre" (Rozenmacher, *Lazarillo* 10).[8]

Of course, the Inquisition was intimately linked to the suppression of Judaism and other nonorthodox Catholic observances in Spain and, subsequently, in Latin America, and it is in this regard that Rozenmacher's play is of interest to this study. In the text that served as the script for the original 1971 production at the IFT, directed by Daniel Figueiredo (a relative, one assumes, of Rozenmacher's wife, Amelia L. Figueiredo, who is credited for her "Asesoramiento literario"), the Jewish theme is present only by oblique reference through the figure of the Inquisidor and the audience's natural familiarity with the connection between the anti-Semitism in the Spanish Empire and the Inquisition, one of whose primary goals was to ferret out and punish those Christians deviating from narrow orthodoxy, including "nuevos cristianos" accused of "Judaizing," that is, continuing to adhere secretly to Jewish customs and observances.

Yet despite the stock features of the Inquisition as a general symbol of the sort of implacable repression of dissidents characteristic of Hispanic culture as, mutatis mutandis, renewed in the right-wing military dictatorships that have been the scourge of modern Argentina, and despite the clear correspondence between the institution of the Inquisition and officially sanctioned anti-Semitism and the persecution of the Jews, the play text itself rarely goes beyond oblique references to a Jewish circumstance. Rather, Rozenmacher appears more directly concerned with the issue of the freedom of the individual and the need to represent the latter's discovery of the bankruptcy of the Counter-Reformation theme of free will so prominent in the culture of the time. This is accomplished through a demonstration of Lazarillo's loss of innocence as regards his "freedom" within the structures of his society, and his acceptance of the imperative to abide by the conditions of survival in his society is the confirmation of this loss of innocence. (The political dimension of Rozenmacher's drama is discussed by Halac; concerning the Jewish elements in the original *Lazarillo de Tormes,* see McGrady).

In the published version of the play, which is certainly partially independent of Figueiredo's production based on Rozenmacher's text, the author complements his explicit interest in the cause of a revolutionary sensibility (one of the essential features of Rozenmacher's writing was the commitment to social revolution, which in the later years of his life meant an identification with the Perónist Left) with direct references to the Jewish resonances of Lazarillo's story, resonances that add another dimension to the anchoring of the play in an Argentine sociopolitical reality:

En alguna medida este tema [de la lucha contra el peso que las generaciones pasadas, que la historia ancestral, desploman sobre nuestra conciencia, impidiéndole así su modificación, su liberación plena como ser humano] es el de la revolución y reaparece en mi manera de sentir el Lazarillo, [porque] ese individuo marginal del 1500, ese *outsider,* era un hombre de origen judío . . . (4; this introduction is entitled "Una propuesta de apertura" [4–6])[9]

It is reasonable to sustain the premise that Rozenmacher's prefatory note is not an appendage to a closed text but an integral part of it as a printed literary document separate, if not completely independent from, the theatrical production. As a printed literary work, Rozenmacher's *El Lazarillo de Tormes,* if it enjoys a contrapuntal relationship to the sixteenth-century novel, also enjoys a tangential relationship to Figuereido's original production. It is a relationship made problematical by Rozenmacher's addition of a prefatory note that to a great degree interprets the work for the reader and adds to it a dimension of sociocultural meaning that seems to be only insinuated in the play's script, which is framed by references to the details of the IFT production. And it is precisely the supplemental nature of the dramatist's note that makes it impossible not to read *El Lazarillo de Tormes* as pertinent to the interests of this study.

Rozenmacher wrote another drama on a Jewish theme, *Simón Brumelstein, el caballero de Indias* (Simón Brumelsten, Knight of the Indies), which was performed posthumously in 1982 at the Teatro Tabarís in Buenos Aires (Senkman 309–16). There is an old joke about the priest and the rabbi discussing hierarchies in the former's religion. The rabbi presses the priest about how a man makes it to the top in the Catholic Church—bishop, cardinal, Pope. When the rabbi asks, "Is that all?" the priest impatiently demands, "Well, what do you expect. For him to get to be Jesus Christ?" The rabbi simply replies, "Well, one of our boys made it." The point is the Christian historical perspective that overlooks how Jesus and other biblical figures were Jews, not Christians (cf. jokes about Mary as a good Jewish daughter and Anne as the paradigmatic Hebrew mother). The result is that Jesus and christological symbolism end up stripped of Jewish roots to become only images of the Son of Man and God incarnate. However, Rozenmacher's *Simón Brumelstein el caballero de Indias* (first performed in 1982, eleven years after the author's death) reinvests Jesus with a Jewish resonance while extending the paschal symbology to include the immolation of a martyr to the tensions within Yiddishkeit and the conflicts between Christians and Jews in the New World.

Rozenmacher's text is extremely complex, as he brings together within the literal and metaphorical space of the theater an array of competing, but simultaneously overlapping, worlds and mentalities, all toward configuring dramatically the almost inevitable psychological fragmentation of the individual in the face of competing demands made upon personal identity in an unrelentingly hostile environment. Rozenmacher's Simón is the focal point for commonplaces concerning the universality of the Jewish persecution, the mendacity of everyday life in the unresolved collision between spiritual values (religious and otherwise) and the raw demands of survival, Jewishness as less a religion than an inward-looking nostalgic refuge from the pressures of the outside, and the psychotic split between the society in which individuals must irremediably live and the fantasies they create in order to assuage the deleterious effects of life in a society they feel to be repugnant and demeaning.

Simón, who believes himself to be a Caballero de Indias related to the first glorious and fantasy-driven—and raving—discoverers of the Americas, rather than the tattered immigrants arriving four centuries later to *hacer la América,* "make it in America," as miserable street vendors and ghetto dwellers, undertakes to escape from history. In the end, he is, as the primary Marxian dogma Rozenmacher knew so well holds, unable to do so, and he is carted off to the mental hospital: "Hay un electroshock, una paliza, una noche y mil noches con aullidos de locos que me esperan" (49),[10] which he realizes full well won't be any different than the real world he has been forced to inhabit. Simón has renounced his secure Jewish world, unable to continue to meet the demands of religion, economic success, and familial responsibility it places on him.

Simón's renunciation is not so much a renunciation of his Jewish identity—in fact, he feels himself to be more Jewish than his carping cousin Katz, who shows up to reproach him for denying his own— as it is an abrogation of conventional responsibility, the repudiation of the "Argentine dream" as it continues to be grasped after by the children and grandchildren of immigrants whose existence is still enveloped in rank dismalness. Simón has sought refuge in what appears to be a boardinghouse as dismal as any in the immigrant ghetto. Simón becomes involved with the wife of the Jew-hating owner of the boardinghouse, and she subscribes to his fantasies, sewing for him the costumes in which he decks himself out as a

Caballero de Indias in order to enact his flight from contemporary society. His room, dominated by a large crucifix that the owner has placed on the wall to remind Simón he is a Jew, becomes the locus for his reveries. Designed without a third wall so that the main space can be invaded on a half-dozen occasions by the figures of Simón's dreams, the set is a metaphor of one individuals's soul, in which various social, religious, and economic structures are overlain to create the effect of schizophrenic chaos as Simón attempts to retain a hold on the unique fantasy he has set out to create for himself: "Si yo no quiero ser judío . . . quiero ser un hombre, nada más." (20).[11]

This set and the boardinghouse room it represents are as much a projection of Simón's inner mind as they are the meeting place for the hellish components of his persecution. Simón is visited by his cousin Katz, who throws in his face how he has had to support Simón's family, accompanied by demands that Simón resume his proper responsibilities. He is visited by Pingitori, his goye lover's anti-Semitic husband, who in the end arranges for Simón to be taken to the mental hospital: "Pero hay normas, hay reglas, uno no puede hacer todo lo que quiere . . . hay familias bien constituidas . . . ¿Por qué usted justo me tuvo que tocar a mí, eh? (40). He is visited by his wife, who has every intention of dragging him back to reality, no matter how dismal it may be for all concerned. And in his fantasies he is visited by his bobe (grandmother), his son, his father, all of whom are figures of the world of Jewish love and convention he has renounced in order to be simply a man by investing himself with the persona of a Caballero de Indias.

The real world Simón inhabits is modern Argentina (cf. the dream sequence on military tyranny and the cattle autocracy [41–43], where all of the myths and dreams of collective success, individual liberty, and social harmony have collapsed). In his fantasies, he inhabits Chantania (derived, undoubtedly, from *chanta*, "black-mailer"), a realm that is both the knightly reverse of the decayed world of history and the extension of it, as it becomes inevitably corrupted by the historical process that turned the mythic and quixotic domain of the conqueror into the contemporary society he inhabits. Thus when Simón agrees to accompany the orderlies from the insane asylum, he demands that they act as his chamberlains and dress him in raiment of his noble order (48–49). The severance of the link between the realm of fantasy and social reality—or, alternately, the definitive contamination of the former by the latter—is signaled by the emergence of the third wall, thereby confining Simón to a historical space from which there is no escape: "*De pronto una tercera pared que durante todo el curso de la obra no existía para dar libertad al mundo de los sueños cae pesadamente cerrando por lateral izquierdo del espectador la pieza, lo que produce un clima asfixiante*" (43).

Simón Brumelstein is Rozenmacher's most complex dramatic work. Like his *Lazarillo* and his by-now classic *Requiem para un viernes a la noche,* it deals with questions of cultural conflict, anti-Semitism, and the stifling nature of Yiddishkeit that is the other face of tight-knit ethnic identity. However, it is Rozenmacher's most metatheatrical piece, in both the multiple meanings assigned to the area of the stage and the ways in which Simón is not only enacting an enforced sociocultural role but also rebelling against it by "improvising" an alternate script. The result is that, with the exception of his lover Guadalupe, who proves unable to protect him, Simón's revised text is acceptable to no one, and the mental illness that is assigned to him is the horrible consequence of his dramatic excesses, which include the fantasy segments he is able to project, but only up to a certain point. It is at that point that Simón's notions of an intrinsic human dignity beyond the mean-spirited ideologies that have circumscribed him collapse, and the unimpeachable, pathetic historical reality of history imposes itself triumphantly.

All that is left for Simón is the no-return escape into complete alienation with no contacts remaining in the external world in which he has suffered: "Curarme . . . ¿de qué? Si estoy en estado de Gracia . . . (*Se acaricia la Cruz.*) Lo que estos nunca sabrán, es que soy un verdadero caballero de Indias . . . y yo voy a sobrevivirlos" (49).[12] As an expression of a commitment to be shared by the audience and Rozenmacher through the figure of Simón to a principle of the primacy of a fantasy that allows one to spurn the depreda-tions of the social dynamic, Simón's words possess an undeniable eloquence. But there is no reason not to believe that the horror of history will remain intact, and a refuge sought in its dankest dungeons may just be the best guarantee that it will, a terrible irony that Rozenmacher's play has no room to resolve.

José Rabinovich (1903–78) was, along with Bernardo Verbitsky (1907–78), one of the most prolific of the Jewish Argentine writers of his generation. Rabinovich was primarily a writer of prose fiction, and his long list of titles explore a variety of topics relating to the immigrant experience in Argentina (Senkman 106–22); some of these titles were written originally in Yiddish, although Rabinovich eventually wrote in Spanish. Rabinovich was particularly suited to deal with these themes, because he was an immigrant himself, having been born in Bialistok and having arrived in Buenos Aires in 1942 (see the autobiographical essay "Penurias" in *El gran castigo* [The Great Punishment] 7–22; Rabinovich published his autobiography as *Sobras de juventud* [Leftovers from My Youth]; cf. also Tiempo, "Treinta preguntas" [Thirty Questions]).

Rabinovich's *Con pecado concebida* (Conceived in Sin) was published in 1975, but, to the best of my knowledge, never performed. Because one of the recurring motifs of the treatment of Jewish experience in Argentine literature concerns mixed marriages and the inevitable trials and tribulations arising from such relationships, this aspect of Rabinovich's play is immediately identified by the reader or presumed spectator.

María is a devout Catholic who has the misfortune to be married to an impotent man who substitutes for the physical love he cannot give her a rather smothering conception of spiritual union. On the first anniversary of their marriage, María accidentally leaves her purse in a taxi; it contains an engraved crucifix that was a wedding gift from her husband. David, the taxi driver, returns her purse to her. The two fall in love, and María leaves her husband for this man, who is a survivor of the Holocaust, and strives to assume something of a Jewish identity as part of their plans to wed. The main action of the play is framed by tableau of María on her deathbed. As she receives Extreme Unction from a priest, she confesses to him that the one sin in her life for which she must atone is having left her husband for a Jew. Between the opening and closing tableaux, the four acts of the play concern the stormy relationship between María and David.

What is notable about *Con pecado concebida* is not specifically its version of the conflict between two lovers, one Christian and one Jew, although this is the thematic substance of the play. Rather, it is Rabinovich's very skillful use of conventions of the modern theater that we generally associate with the theater of the absurd, or at least with a sort of abstract expressionism. The latter conventions involve significant deviations from the highly mimetic or naturalistic evocation of the texture of daily life so characteristic of the bulk of works dealing with social and cultural conflict that have been examined in this study.

One of the salient characteristics of plays by Eichelbaum and Tiempo, written at a time when the Argentine theatergoer had little information about the life of immigrant and other groups outside the mainstream, is the evocation on the stage of lifelike situations the audience can accept as naturalistically verifiable. This quality does not fulfill the criterion of the realistic theater that dramatic situations be lifelike in the sense of something the audience can immediately recognize and with which it can identify in large measure because of the details of the spectator's own experience. Nevertheless, the emphasis on metonymic details of Jewish life in *Pan criollo* or *El judío Aarón* serve to provide an image of "real" life to a presumably interested audience. By contrast, a play such as *Con pecado concebida* highlights circumstantial elements of a realistic nature with abrupt ruptures in dramatic action and shifts in the details of the experiences and emotions being dealt with. As a consequence, there is more of a juxtaposition of nuclear scenes than there is a recognizable trajectory of development of a narrative plot. It is in this way that Rabinovich's play assumes a unique quality as a more complex treatment of the subject of cultural conflict than one associates with slice-of-life treatments that are more the norm in this regard, as witness Eichelbaum's and Tiempo's famous texts.

For example, one of the leitmotifs of the play—and one recalls that such leitmotifs are a distinguishing feature of nonnaturalistic drama and serve to tie together situations and scenes that might otherwise appear unrelated—is the figure of a seedy Jewish cellist who plays the "Kol Nidre" [All the Vows], the prayer recited in the Yom Kippur service in which the supplicant asks for release from all vows undertaken to God and forgiveness for transgressions committed. The cellist plays the "Kol Nidre" as María receives Extreme Unction and confesses her sin, which assumes the proportions of the rejection of Christ. The cellist, during the four acts of the play that recount the relationship between María and David, appears on a number of key occasions, assuming the symbolic status of the incarnation of the fundamental prejudices against Jews that María is never able to overcome (significantly, he is only called the Músico).

The first absurdist rupture in the play comes midway through the first act. María, her husband, and assorted, rather vulgar relatives are assembled to celebrate the couple's first wedding anniversary. María is devastated by the loss of her crucifix; discussion of this misfortune is interrupted by the Músico. It turns out that María is a slum landlady, and the Músico, whom she has threatened with eviction for nonpayment of rent (he has a wife and five children whom he is barely able to support), comes by to tell her that he is on his way to a new job in an orchestra and that, as a consequence, he will be able to pay. María is unreasonably rude over this interruption, and there ensues an ugly scene in which her husband and relatives bait the poor man, oblige him to play for them and then mock his uncreole music. They also insist he drink with them and in general insult him because of his appearance and foreign origins.

Although this is all standard fare in the representation of the most stupid forms of harassment against the cultural outsider, Rabinovich handles it with grotesque elements that demand an explicit theatricality rather than a realistic texture. María and her family become unrelenting furies persecuting the pitiful musician. When the Músico appears subsequently in the play, he may be perceived as an exteriorization of María's deeply ingrained anti-Semitic prejudices and of her emotional discomfiture with Judaism as she struggles with her Catholic identity and her relationship with David. By the same token, as an expressionistic embodiment of the stereotype of the poor and broken Jewish immigrant, the Músico serves also to remind David of his complex ambivalence toward his own Jewish identity, an identity that is all the more vividly highlighted by his involvement with a Catholic woman who loves him but who is fundamentally uncomprehending of and unsympathetic toward his personal suffering.

If *Con pecado concebida* treats María (and her family members, who come and go as a chorus emitting derisive comments about her lover, his ethnic identity, and his difficult nature) as essentially a caricature of certain Argentine views regarding Jews, David is revealed to experience profound conflicts over his ethnic and religious identity. These conflicts derive less from the problems of being a Jew in an often aggressively anti-Semitic society—certainly the issue in so many of the works examined in this study—than from David's doubts concerning God's intentions toward mankind. Rabinovich's works are characterized by what we can in general terms call an existential or Schopenhauerian vision of the individual's struggle in a hostile world. This is certainly the sense of short stories such as those of *Tercera clase,* which I have analyzed elsewhere (Foster, *Argentine Social Realism*). Moreover, one of a series of critical opinions about José Rabinovich that preface *Con pecado concebida* is signed by the celebrated poet Juana de Ibarbourou; it is an opinion that underscores his basic vision of the human condition: En todos los libros de José Rabinovich hay siempre la misma fuerza vital, el mismo dolor de la vida, la misma tremenda rutina gris del destino sin redención de los pobres, la misma sencillez y la misma intensidad. ¡En el teatro qué fuerzas poderosas podría dominar! (7) [13]

Thus the relationship between María and David consists of a series of conversations concerning her confusion over accepting a totally alien, and in many respects repugnant, ethnic tradition. But as a counterpoint to María's difficulties, David articulates his own problems in accepting the principles of his heritage. Their conversations are punctuated at strategic points by appearances of María's relatives to decry her situation and by appearances of figures from David's past who torment him, as the material and external embodiment of the issues that haunt him, about his feelings of rejection toward his Jewishness. Both sets of appearances, those of María's relatives and the figures from David's past, are part of the nonnaturalistic and absurdist texture of the play and lend a fine dramatic sense to the conversations between the two lovers, which might otherwise threaten to become a debate with little theatrical substance (the principal defect of *El gran castigo*).

The title of the play is a trope of the phrase from the Hail Mary prayer: whereas in Catholic doctrine Mary is assigned the quality of having been conceived without sin, both of the paradigmatic human beings in Rabinovich's play are marked by an inescapable human suffering. The burden of this existential, moral, and ethical suffering is for María her torment in the face of cultural traditions with which she is incapable of coming to terms, traditions that include not only the heritage of thousands of years of a unique sense of identity but also the weight of a collective suffering culminating in the Holocaust of which David is a survivor. And, David, because of his experiences in the Holocaust, undergoes profound feelings of rejection of his God, a fact that only complicates María's obviously unsuccessful attempts to comprehend the sense of Jewish identity:

> DAVID.—Dame María, uno o una docena de calmantes. Esos, lo que tú me das, no hacen ya ningún efecto. Necesito algún sendante potente. (*Muy nervioso.*) No existe una habitación, una pieza que no se convierta para mí en una ratonera. Por todos los lados me localiza una abuela o los propios padres. Los padres deben pensar que sus hijos para toda la vida siguen siedo chicos. (61)[14]

> MARIA.— . . . Dios mío, ese hombre sólo me ha llenado la casa con un clima de cementerio. Por donde piso hay un olor a muerte. A la fuerza los judíos introducían en el libro de la vida páginas de desesperación. Como si no podrían [*sic*] existir sin sentirse martirizados. Si no hubieron [*sic*] existido sombras, los judíos las hubieran inventado. (63)[15]

Con pecado concebida is of interest for the nuances of the relationship between David and María, which go beyond the by-now stereotypes of Tiempo's *Pan criollo* or Graiver's *El hijo del rabino,* but what is especially noteworthy about the play is the dramatically convincing use of nonnaturalistic elements. The grotesque and absurdist scenes that punctuate the play frame particular aspects of the cultural conflicts the two protagonists are experiencing and the existential anguish they are undergoing in the face of those conflicts. It is significant that the play leaves unresolved the conflict of that relationship, and that, at the end of the fourth act, there is an abrupt transition from one of David's troubled outbursts back to the opening scene of María receiving Extreme Unction to the strains of the "Kol Nidre" played by the Músico. With *Con pecado concebida,* despite the fact that it seems to have never been performed, Rabinovich achieved a play of compelling dramatic quality.[16]

It would be tempting to characterize the theater of Hebe Serebrisky in terms of the *absurd,* one of the most loosely used terms to describe contemporary Latin American theater (cf. Woodyard). Although it is reasonable to expect to find such a term used to indicate in a very general fashion the coincidences between contemporary works and the post–World War II forms of the theater that had such international influence in the fifties and early sixties, it is nevertheless clear that there is a direct implication that the Spanish-language texts are in some fashion derivative from English- and French-language models. It is for this reason that a major dramatist such as Griselda Gambaro has energetically rejected such a characterization of her work (cf., however, Blanco Amores de Pagella 145–60). Less concerned that she simply be seen as repeating privileged European and American works, Gambaro is in reality far more preoccupied that *absurd* indicate that her works and those of her fellow dramatists transcend the conflicts of everyday life in order to deal with the metaphysical abstraction implied by the adjective (Gambaro 7–20 and 21–37).

Of course, Gambaro insists, the fact is quite to the contrary: what may superficially appear to be metaphysically absurd plots, situations, dialogues, and use of physical space of the stage are, in fact, theatrical metaphors for very immediate and palpable realities of Latin American life. The structures of oppression and repression, of persecution and aggression, of arbitrary exploitation and gratuitous cruelty are such an inherent part of daily life in even a putatively sophisticated city such as Buenos Aires that the human relations expressed in *Los siameses* (The Siamese Twins), *El desatino* (The Blunder), and *El campo* (The Camp) are not absurdist abstractions but "realistic" situations given the heightened quality of theatrical expression.

It is for this reason that it is not critically sound, when pursuing a topic like "Jewish themes in Argentine drama," to rely on a distinction between those works that treat the factual outlines of the subject in a documentary, straightforward, or explicit fashion and those works in which the sociocultural issue at hand attains a complex metaphoric elaboration. Certainly dramatists such as Samuel Eichelbaum, César Tiempo, José Rabinovich, and Germán Rozenmacher, because of the theatrical conventions within which they were working, offer particularly obvious representations of situations and conflicts and encourage audience interpretation in an unambiguous fashion. To be sure, one can assume that recent theater, which is characterized by especially complex metathetical features, no longer deals with the questions of daily social life, and therefore, it does not encourage audience interpretation in an unambiguous fashion. Gambaro, however, is someone who repudiates emphatically such an assumption, as does a significant inventory of Argentine dramatists; one of the standard works on contemporary Argentine theater underscores the quality of "realism" at issue here (Tirri).

Enthusiastically endorsed by Griselda Gambaro, Serebrisky's dramas exemplify this point. Their affiliation with the absurd seems necessary for Graciela M. Peyrú to establish—"El absurdo sin límites crea en Hebe Serebrisky sus propias reglas" (Peyrú, in Serebrisky 7) [17]—but it is obvious that this quality means not that they deal with metaphysical abstractions but rather, in conformance with Gambaro's own example, with the confusing or "absurdizing" reality of daily experiences. The dominant feature of Serebrisky's dramas is an interest in interpersonal relationships, the games of power and control that individuals exercise over one another, and both the strategies of aggression and the strategies of compensation that such undertakings involve.

A nucleus of neorealist dramatists in Argentina, including

Roberto Cossa, Ricardo Halac, Carlos Gorostiza, and Carlos Somigliana, have dealt with these themes by repeating on the stage the gestures of our daily experience, in conformance with the metathetrical conventions that currently prevail—the absurdist conventions in a very broad sense. By contrast, Serebrisky—like Gambaro, Osvaldo Dragún, Eduardo Pavlovsky, and Ricardo Monti—shuns the transparently meaningful theatrical gestures in favor of complex expressionistic schemes. These are often what is really being referred to in the use of a term that has gained considerable currency in Argentina, the *grotesque*. The latter designation is particularly valuable because of its implications about the quality of human experience evoked on the stage.

The preceding comments are necessary in order to frame adequately a play such as Serebrisky's *Don Elías campeón* (Don Elías the Champion), which was performed in late 1980 at Buenos Aires's Teatro Municipal General San Martín, technically one of the most elaborate theatrical complexes on the continent. The play centers on Don Elías, who is approximately sixty-five years old. The son of Rumanian immigrants, Elías owns a small general store in a deadened provincial town. His father was an itinerant peddler, and he is married to a pragmatic skeptic whose eternal lament is her husband's dreamy distractions. The couple's son, Abel, who eschewed a career in classical music in order to play the violin in an itinerant tango band, is killed with his wife at a railroad crossing. Don Elías and Zulema assume the burden of their three children, and the play is, in the fashion of Argentine literature on the customs of daily life, filled with allusions to both the practices and the concerns of day-to-day experience. It is thus possible to underscore in a fairly straightforward fashion motifs prominent in a certain type of art in immigrant culture in Argentina: a first- or second-generation family whose names, customs, and conversation evoke in varying degrees their noncreole origins and, as a result, their oblique relationship to the omnipresent Argentine myths of national cultural unity; a trajectory of dramatic action that involves a form of sociocultural conflict related to this oblique relationship; and a form of theatrical rhetoric that encourages the audience to interpret the consequences of such a situation.

In the case of *Don Elías campeón,* the dramatic action turns on the quality of Elías as a "champion." Don Elías is a champion of *generala,* an Argentine creole version of poker, dice, or yahtze. For thirty years he has been the undefeated *generala* champion, and his entire social interaction with the world seems to focus on this game, much to the despair of Zulema, for whom *generala* is of inconsequence in the face of economic necessities, keeping the store, and raising three grandchildren. As a first approximation to the definition of Elías's cultural value in the play, we therefore may underscore how the son of an itinerant Jewish peddler builds his personal identity on being the town champion of a paradigmatically creole pastime.

Nevertheless, the references to *generala* are intersected by another important cultural element in the play, Don Elías's attachment to classical music, specifically to the performances of Yasha Heifitz. When Elías is not engaged in the local bar playing *generala* with his cronies and defending his championship, he is cradled in the arms of his easy chair, in the back rooms of his general store, listening to his music while his wife bustles in yenta rumblings around him.

These two dominant cultural references come together in allusions to the absent beloved son, from whose horrible death the father has been unable to recover psychologically. Although he spurned the paternal model by both escaping the general store and substituting for the classical music of the Old Country what to Elías's ears is the tinny music of the Argentine tango—substituting symbolically the violin of a Heifitz for a creole fiddle—Abel for both parents naturally represents the ideal of their family life. His death and the irresolvable conflicts of their life underscore how the absent son, who can only be evoked vaguely and in the context of intense personal suffering and conflict, indicates to them the discontinuities of their existence.

Abel's death, which has occurred before the beginning of the play and which colors all of the interrelationships between the characters and their actions, serves as an eloquent metaphor for the frustrations and failures of a social dynamic. Although the text indicates a tender relationship between Elías and Zulema, it is an uncharacteristic respite in their daily conflicts. Elías's two cultural points of reference, *generala* and classical music, are sources of conflict for him, both in his own home and in his dealings with the townspeople, who respect his championship but who do not have any affection for him. The controlling theatrical detail of *Don Elías campeón* is the homemade "altar" to his personal interests: the arm chair in which he listens to music; his stereophonic equipment; the table on which he keeps the *generala* dice, shaking cup, and score pad; and the portrait of his deceased son. The play most breaks with the conventions of naturalistic theater in its handling of this axis for the dramatic action of the play. Dream or fantasy sequences that provide an expressionistic counterpoint to the realistic representation of Elías's personal conflicts involve transformations of these basic props. For example, the following two sets of instructions mark the transition from the first to the second scenes of the play (there are seven altogether): Trastienda de un típico negocio de pueblo provinciano en el que se vende tela, ropa, lencería, mercería. A izquierda, un cortinado de terciopelo azul desteñido marca la separación con la tienda. Salvo ese detalle incongruente, el decorado, de muebles antiguos, denota una sólida posición económica. A foro derecha, otra puerta, comunica directamente con la calle. Sillón de un cuerpo con apoyabrazos. Atrás, cuelga la enorme fotografía del rostro de un muchacho, retocada estilo pintura. A derecha, mesa con cuatro sillas, aparador de cristales y fondo de espejo arriba. Delante del sillón, suntuoso tocadiscos de pie, estereofónico. Otra puerta, comunica con la cocina y demás habitaciones. (45)[18]

Luz anaranjada baña todo el escenario. Suena muy suave un solo de violín. Don Elías está sentado en una especie de trono que en realidad no es más que su sillón elevado del suelo por una plataforma con forma de cubilete: cilindro más ancho arriba que abajo en cuero repujado. Hugo está parado frente a Don Elías con los brazos cruzados. Lo interroga muy curioso. (50)[19]

In addition to Elías and Zulema, there are two other characters in the work, Antonio and Hugo. Antonio, the gatekeeper of the railroad crossing, brought the news to Elías that his son's vehicle had been rammed by a train. Since that time a bond has developed between the two men that Zulema objects to but finds herself helpless to break. A marginal symbol of law and order (in some of the dream sequences, Antonio's uniform becomes his defining feature), the expressionistic symbolism of the play implies that he is the external or material representation of the forces of conflict and disharmony, of the "algo que anduvo muy mal," that haunts Elías with reference to both his own cultural position and his relationship with his son. When Antonio is rejected by Elías at the end of the play, he utters the classic Argentine anti-Semitic epithet, "¡Ruso de mierda!" (85),[20] and it would be legitimate for the spectator to see Antonio, in the mundane terms of sociocultural causes and effects, as the grasping and opportunistic creole anxious to take advantage of the psychologically troubled and distracted Elías.

Hugo, on the other hand, is the token for another creole stereotype in the artistic versions of immigration in Argentina. The son of a local woman of dubious virtue and of a missing father, Hugo was a sometime friend of Abel's. Obviously, in a schematic fashion, Hugo represents the inversion of the figure of Abel as the controlling metaphor of the play: he is present and it is his father, who confers on him the paradigmatic status of *guacho* ("abandoned," "fatherless [without identity]," "bastard"), who is the absent figure. It is only natural for Elías and Hugo to form a relationship that is both a corrective to the Elías-Antonio axis and a restoration of the broken Elías-Abel one. At the end of the play, when Hugo (who seems to constitute the only real threat in thirty years to Elías's status as *generala* champion) agrees to become Elías's figurative son and the heir to his general store, a personal and social equilibrium is achieved that provides a sense of conclusion.

If one characterizes Serebrisky's play simply in terms of a value assigned to the individual characters or to specific actions in the play and to the props used, there would appear to be little deviation from the long inventory of Argentine works dealing with the Jewish immigrant experience in terms of very explicit and transparent references to the details, to the realia of day-to-day life. What is "absurd"—expressionistic, grotesque, nonnaturalistic—about *Don Elías campeón* is how what appear to be realistic details are transformed into theatrically abstract and ambiguous signs that forestall approaching the issues of social, psychological, and cultural dynamics in the play as material that has to be "acted out" in a very similar fashion using languages that are comfortable extensions of what we accept as the details of the real world. There is a degree of presence of these languages in Serebrisky's play (although one is relieved to find no folkloristic Yiddishized talk). But it is precisely the ruptures—especially in the scenes dealing with the conflicting relationship between Elías and Antonio on the one hand and between Elías and Hugo on the other—with realistic convention in favor of more complex theatrical metaphors that most give freshness to the dramatist's interpretation of a set of abiding themes in Argentine culture.

Jorge Goldenberg (1941) has received considerable attention as an outstanding Argentine representative of the so-called documentary theater, particularly for *Relevo 1923*, which won Havana's prestigious Casa de las Américas Prize in 1975. Although the play refers to events involving Argentina's famed anarchist movements, in which many Jews were involved, *Relevo 1923* does not concern itself with questions of Jewish identity.

Krinsky does, however. Awarded the 1983 Primer Premio Bienal de Teatro, sponsored by Union Carbide Argentina, *Krinsky* is an interpretation of a childhood memory of the author. In his introduction, "Prólogo: el otro Krinsky" (Prologue: The Other Krinsky), Goldenberg recalls Adolfo Krinsky as a town character or eccentric of San Martín, the city in the province of Buenos Aires in which Goldenberg grew up. A Russian immigrant, Krinsky served as librarian of the local Jewish center and as an itinerant photographer. There were many stories and controversies surrounding both activities. Krinsky was also a poet, in both Spanish and Yiddish, and when his body was found several days after his death in his rundown bachelor apartment, old one-peso notes were found sewn into the lining of the tattered and grimy overcoat he always wore. Goldenberg recalls that speculation was divided between whether these notes were part of a meager hoard of worthless money or whether they served to provide his garment with additional insulation.

As a childhood memory tinged with the selective emphases of the recollection of the past and the nostalgic aureola of regret over the loss of the points of reference of that childhood, the figure of Krinsky serves for Goldenberg as a personal image of the disappearance of a version of Jewish folk culture in Argentina. Although the work has yet to be performed, it is not unreasonable to assume that part of the prologue might appear as a program note, thereby establishing for the spectator the link between the explicit text of the play and the personal motives of the dramatist in writing it (an added dimension is the fact that the play was begun during Goldenberg's absence from Argentina, and it is first dated in Caracas, 1977).

The explicit text of the play is a series of vignettes that center on the apparently daily visit by Krinsky to the corner grocery story of Luba. It is clear that Krinsky hangs out around the store and is accustomed to begging for scraps of food from Luba, who is alternately happy to have him as company and upset over his many eccentricities, his unkempt appearance, and his constant challenges to Luba's petit-bourgeois mercantilism. The setting for the action of the play is Luba's store, and the main line of dialogue consists of the squabbling between the two of them: Krinsky accuses her of being insensitive to his interests and concerns in her obsession over maintaining the small business, and Luba berates Krinsky over his appearance and his eternal whining. But *Krinsky* is more than a dialogue between two older persons whose individual and combined concerns and eccentricities, as verbalized in the complex pattern of their conversation, might be taken as bespeaking some form of collective identity. The naturalism of this basic line of the text's organization is broken by a series of parentheses that represent incursions into the space Luba and Krinsky inhabit of materializations of elements of their past. It is mostly Krinsky's past, but to the extent that they share a common cultural heritage, it becomes to a great extent the identity that Krinsky is committed to sustaining and that Luba is indifferent about remembering. In succession, like the ghosts of Jewish life past and present, they are visited by the Cosaco, who represents Krinsky's involvement with the Russian Revolution and the promise of the latter to overcome the conflicts of racial and religious identity; Harpo Marx, one embodiment of Jewish culture beyond the ghetto; the Madre, an amalgam of Krinsky's real mother and a mythic Jewish maternal force; the Actor, another embodiment of Jewish culture, this time specifically the provincial Eastern European Yiddish comedy that had extensive projections in Argentina; two Esbirros who are the tragic obverse of the burlesque tradition in their incarnation of anti-Semitism and, more specifically, Argentine thugs who lived by the slogan "Haga patria, mate un judío"[21] (Viñas describes these sentiments in *En la semana trágica*); and, finally, the gentile Muchacha, an idealization of the feminine love Krinsky never had (Luba throws in Krinsky's face the cruel joke of the town's people that, in his profession as a photographer, his bed has held all of the prettiest girls in town—in the form of positives laid out to dry).

These images of Krinsky's identity appear in successive fashion as both a consequence of the patter between him and Luba and as the source of further contention. At the close of the play, they reemerge as a chorus to accompany Krinsky's humble death, the death of a lonely and seedy man ("nuestra vida solo vale un escupitajo,"[22] according to the quote from one of Krinsky's own poems; 9), but a man who nevertheless doggedly persisted in being a spokesman for a tradition of collective memory and identity.

The fundamental conflict between Krinsky and Luba is over the value of this memory and identity. Luba accepts the elements of her culture as something that is just there, but over which no big deal is to be made. By contrast, for her, Krinsky is obsessed by them, and, of course, the materialization of the representative figures is an expressionistic confirmation of the degree of this obsession. The play raises the question in a number of ways as to whether the past is worth remembering, with all its trivialities and misery. Krinsky's death, which occupies about a third of the text, is the death of this past, and the chorus of the figures of his memory represents both its complexity and the contradictions of its utility. The Actor's advice to Krinsky refers as much to the insignificance of Krinsky's seemingly futile existence as it does to the ethnic heritage Krinsky evokes through the former and the other figures: "En mi opinión, lo mejor que podrías hacer ahora es conseguirte una buena muerte" (60).[23] Throughout, Luba treats Krinsky as an old rag that gets in the way of her incessant cleaning, an object to be discarded as useless and offensive; at one point she literally picks him up by his ragged clothes and shoves him out of the way. At another point, the voices of the two become categorically antiphonic:

KRINSKY *(al público)*.—¡Mírenla, por favor! [a la Muchacha]

LUBA *(al público)*.—Olvídense . . . olvídense . . . ¿Para qué acordarse? (56) [24]

In centering on the figure of Krinsky and the pathos of his death at the end (when, of course, when it is too late, Luba confesses to hearing the past she had earlier denied [68]), Goldenberg unequivocably extols the complex of values the poet-photographer-librarian represents.

As a text addressed to an audience, there are two features of *Krinsky* that bear special mention. Like all dramatic works, the play is constructed to be "received" by an audience, whether or not the spectators are specifically addressed by the characters. In the case of Goldenberg's play, the public is constantly appealed to by the actors, much in the homey way in which a third party is appealed to by the participants in a heated discussion. Thus the audience of *Krinsky* is asked explicitly to take sides in the debate between Krinsky and Luba in the first instance, and between Krinsky and the images of his memory in the second instance. To a great degree, this feature challenges the audience in a more overt sense than the simple challenge to accept or reject offered by any discourse addressed to it by implication. Rather, the audience must take sides in the argument between Krinsky and Luba, to *mirar* or to *olvidar*. To the extent that spectators remain in the theater, they accept Krinsky's order by default to *mirar*.

The other feature of interest here is also a challenge to the audience, this time in the form of linguistic elements. Much Yiddish is used in the play, which Goldenberg translates in appended foot notes. In terms of the dramatic dialogue of the characters, either they translate for each other or they paraphrase what has been said. The challenge is less for a gentile audience to comprehend Yiddish, because one can reasonably presume that the audience does not know the language, than for the Lubas of the audience to accept and to understand the lingua franca of their culture. Krinsky and the other characters do not resort to Yiddish because they do not know Spanish—the Harpo Marx of Krinsky's memory, of course, speaks it with native fluency—but because recourse to Yiddish is dictated by particular sentiments or values being expressed. It is well known that in cases of true bilingualism, the two languages are complementary rather than overlapping, and code switching from one language to the other is dictated by the circumstances of the discourse, with one language covering one set of features and the other language an opposite or contrary one (cf. Lipsky). Note as a consequence Krinsky's direct statement, referring to the audience and his use of terms and phrases in Yiddish, "No se dan cuenta de nada porque no entienden idisch" (31).[25] This affirmation is a correlative both of the audience's separation from a culture that is not their own and which they have historically rejected (the stereotyped reaction to Jewish culture on the part of dominant Argentine self-identity) and the degree to which a Jewish audience accepts the form of collective memory defended by Krinsky in his moving obsessions.

Jewish writers in Argentina may no longer feel the need to concern themselves exclusively with themes of ethnic identity, although many of them continue to do so: Mario Goloboff, Ricardo Feierstein, Alicia Steimberg, and Marcos Aguinis are only a few such writers. Because the 1980s marked the centennial of the establishment of Jewish colonies in Argentina and the arrival of an impressive contingent of Jewish immigrants as part of the Argentine policy of immigration at that time, works like Goldenberg's *Krinsky* play an important role in commemorating this important aspect of Argentine social history and the complex of cultural issues surrounding it.

The works examined in this chapter represent not a survey of Argentine dramatic works dealing with the Jewish experience but a detailed commentary on a few selected texts that represent more various types of theatrical strategies for dealing with the subject than simply a constellation of themes. Theater is a complicated form of cultural representation, and Argentina has been one of the leading countries in South America in the development of dramatic forms to represent its complex national culture. The works studied here represent well the various types of theater to be found in that country. Certainly Eichelbaum, who wrote *Nadie la conoció nunca* and

El judío Aarón early in his career exemplifies the thesis drama that dominated before the Teatro Independiente movement. Social and cultural issues are represented in a naturalistic fashion, one that is recognizable to an audience whose own experiences overlap with those of the characters. The play moves toward a well-defined conclusion about an issue, and there can be little doubt as to the way in which "real life" is duplicated on the stage.

With the Teatro Independiente movement beginning in the early 1930s, although one still finds a considerable adherence to identifiable issues, there is a greater concern for experimentation with the theatrical space and with projecting an image of the theater as a conceitful metaphor of life rather than merely its documentary recreation. Thus Tiempo's *El teatro soy yo* combines a thesis about human relations with a metatheatrical postulate that equates human behavior with a theatrical representation in a way that demands that we be as concerned with the nature of theater as we are with the thesis involved.

Finally, in the works by Rabinovich (especially a more convincing drama such as *Con pecado concebida*), Rozenmacher, and Serebrisky, various elements of the grotesque, the absurd, and the expressionistic attest to a conception of the theater whereby dramatic action defies a naturalistic norm in order to frame elements taken from the context of human experience in a way that allows their contemplation or examination from various overlapping perspectives. Rather than relying on a recreation of immediately identifiable social life, these works reflect a conception of the problematics of the interpretation of human experience through a mosaic of juxtapositions, abrupt shifts of perspective, and highly foregrounded metaphoric signs that do not lend themselves to facile explanations. The consequence of such a "difficult" theater is that the spectator is urged to consider both the hard-to-define nature of the forms of life being represented and the irresolvable conflicts depicted.

Surely, then, one cannot speak of these works by offering interpretations of Jewish culture in Argentina: these plays cannot be reduced to any correspondence with sociologically or politically defined propositions. Should one wish to do so, their specific theatrical quality must be overlooked. By examining each text in considerable detail for its dramatic and theatrical structure, the goal has been to promote the sense of their importance as cultural documents rather than as mere repositories of thematic motifs that can only be (re)interpreted in terms of postulates. Of course, these works deal with sociopolitical postulates and often with ones that are quite obvious. But the principal concern of this investigation has been to maintain the importance of seeing those postulates in terms of dramatic and theatrical issues that both frame and set the limits of the ways in which they may be interpreted as cultural documents. It is only in this way that we may respect the artistic conventions within which they were written while recognizing their importance as Argentine social texts.

In organizing this chapter, I have basically made use of all existing dramatic texts by Jewish authors, with the exception of material that either exists in archival fashion or, although a bibliographical reference is available, I have not been able to locate (cf. Foster and Lindstrom). In this sense, my representation is certainly not selective, and the arrangement of the discussion is roughly chronological. Therefore, there are few interpretive conclusions to be drawn from the juxtaposition of one text to another, beyond what I have already stated above.

However, I would like to close by returning to the question of theater as a cultural genre. One need make little argument for the special sociocultural position of the theater in our society, whether from the unique role of theater as spectacle or from its importance at certain historical points in the collective enterprise of group definition along various societal axes. I think the important point to be made about the participation of Jewish artists in the theater in Argentina, a participation that continues to be significant whether or not specifically Jewish themes or issues are involved, concerns access by representatives of a particular group within Argentine society to the public display of culture. Early immigrant groups in Argentina and their children tended to reduplicate the inward-oriented life of either the village shetl or the urban ghetto, in a combination of enforced separation and separation by choice dictated by multiple social and economic pressures, which are also a form of enforced separation. In this sense, Argentine Jews were essentially no different than other immigrant groups in Argentina and immigrant groups in general in the New World. The emergence in the context of immense economic prosperity following World War I of numerous popular culture formats in the twenties and thirties—radio, movies, pulp magazines, dance-hall culture—played an influential role in mainstreaming an entire range of socially definable subclasses in a dynamic, urbanized world like that of Buenos Aires. And although theater was already a traditional high-culture genre, along with other high-culture productions it benefitted from the openings that took place during the golden age in question. High-culture genres left the drawing rooms, select clubs, and academic forums and mingled with popular modes as part of a vast process of cultural democratization that began to take place in the 1920s and that has continued to be one of the hallmarks of Argentine society. Although Jewish artists and Jewish culture can be traced in large segments of the production that emerges at this time, one of my points throughout this chapter has been the privilege of the theater in showcasing, in a highly public space and as a highly prized cultural genre, matters of particular interest to the Jewish collectivity. By the extension of successfully placing these matters before a public that was no longer exclusively Jewish (as was, say, the audience of the old Yiddish-language stage), Jewish dramatists began the long process, still incomplete in many respects, of intertwining their own identities with the complex fabric of Argentine social life. There is no reason to believe that the theater was a necessarily efficient vehicle for this process, but the fact is, quite simply, as the works studied here demonstrate, an involvement of Jewish dramatists with the Argentine theater has provided the study of Jewish culture in Argentina with an especially significant inventory of artistic production.

⊷ CONCLUSIONS ⊶

Because this collection of essays has been pursuing neither a guiding theme nor a unifying methodology, I can offer no conclusions
that would lead the reader back to Latin American literature via a
synthesizing perspective. Indeed, it would not be inappropriate for
one to believe that I have aspired to nothing more than a selective
mosaic of topics that reflect my personal enthusiasms of the moment.
Yet I would insist that there are unifying bases for these chapters,
and that, although they do characterize my own critical agenda,
they point, persuasively I would hope, to an expanded format for
Latin American literary studies in this country. It is probably preten-
tious to seek to relate these issues to highly resonant terms such as
subaltern studies and *postcolonial criticism,* but work in these two
overlapping fields has heavily influenced my thinking about Latin
American literature, even if it is not always apparent because of the
ways in which the scholar inevitably reduplicates the blindnesses of
his (the pronoun is meant to be specific and not generic) formation
and positioning.

A commitment to subalternity emerges whenever one undertakes
to question the hegemonic. In this case, it has meant more than an
interest in feminist writing, an interest that has firmly established
itself in Hispanic studies and enriched our reading immeasurably. I
could have chosen to reflect this interest by offering additional feminist readings, as I have done in my various interpretations of writing
in the context of recent Argentine military dictatorships and the subsequent period of redemocratization. But the subalternity of feminist

voices and their antiphonic status vis-à-vis the masculinist dominant can profitably be intersected with other dimensions of subalternity. Thus I have sought to characterize a lesbianism where subalternity is doubled because it is both feminist and counterheterosexist, reminding the reader that patriarchal structures are both antifeminist and (as a consequence of their very dynamic) compulsively heterosexist.

Walsh's prose, which, although she has written "adult" poetry, is marked by its being addressed to an implied child reader, brings to the fore the potential for intervening in the processes of subject formation at an early age: whereas most feminist writing seeks to restructure already formed consciousnesses or to bring out submerged, repressed identities, a feminist children's writing, of which there is still markedly little to analyze, portrays notably successful efforts—in Walsh's case, of undertaking the project of alternative consciousness even within the context of military tyranny. What is particularly eloquent in Walsh's case is that a large portion of her works were written, published, and widely consumed during some of the darkest years for constitutional institutions and human rights in Argentina, and, as apparently the military censors where unable to notice, Walsh's texts undermine in several crucial ways the "Western, Judeo-Christian family values" that were the (often incoherent) ideological underpinnings of their authority and the appeal to public legitimation. Children were perhaps the most devastated victims of the tyranny, a point that Luis Puenzo's 1985 film *La historia oficial* (The Official Story) sought to demonstrate, and the fact that the film leaves unresolved the fate of the little girl, Gaby, is less a case of the film's waffling over the historical issues involved than it is an index of how Argentine society had (has) yet to resolve the conflicts created for these children. Significantly, both Puenzo's film and Walsh's books are examples of popular culture materials that have been tremendous commercial successes. Walsh has reached a large audience, and although more rigorous feminist agendas might wonder about how effective her writing may ultimately be, my analysis of it suggests that it is sustained by a coherent attitude of contestation well in conformance with the imperative to shatter stifling paternalist attitudes.

Finally, although I cannot make much of a case for a specific femi-

nist consciousness among Argentine-Jewish theater production—
there is much more to be found among poets and novelists, for
example, Alejandra Pizarnik and Alicia Steimberg, respectively—
women's subalternity must surely intersect with the profound subalternity of Jewishness in Argentina, whether viewed against the
backdrop of that country's Catholic heritage (which, although it
may not be manifest in public ritual as it is, say, in Mexico, is undoubtedly there as a master narrative repeatedly evoked by right-
wing government, especially military ones) or viewed in terms of a
social dynamic whereby the Jew is the convenient scapegoat as the
distinctive Other. Serebrisky brings a specifically feminist viewpoint
to the fore in her plays, but it is there, if only rather condescendingly,
in the plays by Eichelbaum, Tiempo, and Rozenmacher. (I note that
Jewishness and feminism intersect in the novel by the Mexican Levi
Calderón.)

Postcolonialist criticism, on the other hand, is what has allowed
me to seek out those topics that consistently fall outside our class-
room teaching of Latin America and, regrettably, so much of our
published research. Since the 1960s there has been a growing di-
versification in Latin American cultural studies, spurred most immediately by the geometrically increasing numbers of scholars and
the necessarily different points of view they bring with them to
their teaching and research. Both the Cuban Revolution and Central American conflicts have provided contexts for dramatic shifts
of critical interest, and the inescapable historical necessities of the
military regimes in the Southern Cone have been a point of departure for drawing renewed interpretive undertakings. However, there
are three perspectives directly related to a postcolonial mentality
that I have drawn upon in these essays that I feel deserve special
encouragement. The first is the need to incorporate Brazil into the
realm of a truly Latin American critical discourse. *Latin American* and *Spanish American* are often used interchangeably. Where
the latter specifically excludes Brazil (and Haiti, for that matter), it
usually masks the fact that *Latin* is accepted as synonymous with
Spanish. There are many persuasive reasons not to homogenize Brazil into the rest of Latin America, just as, for that matter, there are
many persuasive reasons not to homogenize the Spanish American

republics (the Andean, Central American, and Southern Cone ones) into a Pan-American consensus. But despite enormous differences, Brazil is part of a common destiny of Latin America, and there are as many continuities as dissonances between Spanish-language and Portuguese-language based cultures, beginning with the fact that Spanish American literature is extensively read in translation in Brazil, even if Brazilian literature is not read as much in Spanish translation. But common sociopolitical circumstances, imposed as much by international capitalist imperialism as by shared historical antecedents, renders it artificial if not senseless to continue to exclude Brazil from our thinking about Latin America or to continue to treat it as a supplement or appendix. The refusal of American Latin Americanists (except, of course, for specifically Brazilianists) to learn Portuguese and to study Brazilian cultural production is the colonist side of the coin, which is why strategies for the nonspecial-case incorporation of Brazil into criticism can lay a certain claim to being postcolonialist.

Perhaps it is the special-case scenario that is most at issue here. Puig's homoerotic sensibility, if it is mentioned at all, is customarily treated as a special case. Indeed, the willingness to silence what is gay about Puig's writing derives from, in my opinion, an appalling view that any showcasing of queer perspectives is special pleading on the part of the author or the critic, a version of the disastrous liberal view that everything must be universalized so that concrete manifestations of sexual desire—certainly ones that are so concrete as to be disturbingly deviant, however deviance is calculated—must be drowned in the generalizing appeal to the motif of the victim, abstracted as the Victim, or rendered as allegories of the political, whereby the substance of the allegory is set aside in favor of what it is "really" supposed to mean. Insisting on charting the specifics of homoerotic desire in Latin American cultural production strives to fend off the liberal, typically American, ethos of interpretive abstraction: the reduction of semantic details to motifs that are safe because they have been naturalized: political persecution but not lesbian bashing.

But there is a second dimension of postcolonialist criticism involved here, and that is the effort that needs to be expended, once one has accepted the legitimacy of dealing with something like homoeroticism as such, in order to not interpret that dimension of Latin American cultural production in American or European terms—or, for that matter, not to interpret it in Pan-American terms. The bugaboo of political correctness might prove useful here: Mattoso's sex manual certainly represents one outrageous entry in Latin American opposition to a normalized heterosexism (as it involves both homoeroticism and deviant heterosexism), but it would likely be deemed politically incorrect if it were a contemporary American text, beginning with its reinscription of sadomasochistic motifs. It may make a lot of sense to speak of treating these works "on their own terms," but it is not always clear how one can escape the immediate practice of applying foreign models to the corpus: indeed, to use those foreign models to define the corpus. One alternative would be to back away from the privileging of a lesbian or gay identity for a block of Latin American cultural production, in line with arguing that sexual preference is less a matter of identity politics in Latin America than it is in the United States. This might run the risk of silencing once again the homoerotic, although it would occur in a context quite different from what I see as the silencing of the homoerotic in criticism on Puig and so many others. Obviously, I have chosen to continue to frame something like a gay sensibility, while always trying to see ways in which it does not reinvent with a Latin American tinge U.S. or European models and always trying to avoid the mere reading of the texts in terms of a hegemonic theoretical bibliography.

The existence of the Latin American Jewish Studies Association attests to the way in which there is now a considerable inventory of critical studies on Latin American Jews and their cultural production, so perhaps I can plead less establishment transgressions in this matter. Yet the emphasis has been on social history and on reading literary works as primarily social history. I am more concerned with the specific discourse strategies associated with a public spectacle like theater and with the problematical advantages available to public spectacle, as opposed to "private" poetry and narrative. Drama stages personal and interpersonal conflict in a public space with inescapably present and real human bodies. This does not make theater a more "eloquent" form of cultural production, but it does make it one of a notably different social register. Much like homoeroticism, Jewishness is often either submerged in a gesture of universalizing interpretation or it is viewed as special pleading. If there is anything postcolonial about my treatment of a fairly wide array of texts, it is in the insistence on seeing them as an integral part of the Argentine theatrical tradition and, moreover, as seeing that during a significant period of its development, the Argentine stage has always had a marked Jewish presence about it. I don't pretend to have demonstrated this conclusively, but rather only to have begun the work that this topic requires, which is all I would say about the other dimensions of this book: the examination of writing for children, the charting of homoerotic sexuality, and the merits of seeing these dimensions in ways that include an always-vigorous Brazilian cultural production.

⊷⊜ NOTES ⊜⊷

CHAPTER I. SPANISH AMERICAN
AND BRAZILIAN LITERATURE

1. It is always necessary to clarify that modernism in Brazil refers to a literary, cultural, and artistic movement paralleling ideologically and chronologically the modernist vanguard of Europe and the United States. Therefore, it should not be confused with Spanish American *modernismo,* the cultural equivalent of late nineteenth century European liberalism, heavily influenced by French Parnassianism and symbolism. Although it has been suggested that Spanish American *modernismo* and Brazilian modernism (its Latin American parallel is called *vanguardismo*) are continuous, Latin American historiography insists on distinguishing between the two, if for no other reason than a chronological one.

CHAPTER II. SOME PROPOSALS

1. In *Gay and Lesbian Themes* (87–93), I have analyzed the intersection between transvestism and homosexual desire in a brothel setting as signs of patriarchal violence and social control in the Chilean José Donoso's *El lugar sin límites* (1966). There is a superb 1977 film version of Donoso's novel by the Mexican filmmaker Arturo Ripstein. I discuss the question of homosexual representation in the Argentine Manuel Puig's *Beso de la mujer araña* (1976), but with specific reference to Héctor Babenco's 1985 film version, *Kiss of the Spider Woman* (Foster, *Narrativity in Contemporary Argentine Cinema,* pp. 123–135). The Latin American writer who in his fiction has most incorporated transvestism, in its multiple meanings and dimensions, is Cuba's Severo Sarduy. This aspect of Sarduy's work has yet to receive anything like the analysis it deserves.

2. He is out in the backyard. It is night. Everyone is asleep. The light blanches things—stones, the bottom of tin cans, his hands. And *that thing* comes over him, that thing seizes him, and suddenly it makes him feel superior, strong, alone, and terribly, terribly wretched. . . . He is out in the country. He is a boy. From the arbor he can hear the voices of his relatives talking near the back door of his house as

they hoe weeds among the corn. They are the familiar, soothing voices that carry on the ordinary conversations of every day. But there is something behind them, underneath them, underneath those words—something that only he understands; and every word, every sound changes into a sort of challenge, a dare, a terror, a possibility of tenderness an enigma, *his* enigma, for only he is allowed to understand it. But what must he do? Who must he go to—if, indeed, there is anyone in this town that can guide him . . . He is in the dining room, in the house in town. The radio is playing some popular song, some stupid, ordinary song, one of those songs his cousin Esther likes so much. And there, too, there is some urgent, demanding thing, a thing that commands him, transports him, a thing that lifts him and carries him away, and that leaves him with a [*sic*] myriad doubts and questions, questions different from those that the common days of life bring on . . . And now he is the condemned man, now the chosen one, the man who will not fit in, the man who will not conform, the man who possesses a horror which will not be held to the narrow limits of daily misery. He is the man who cannot listen to a song and say, *I hear a song*—and let that be it. The man who cannot listen to some familiar conversation and tell himself, *I hear people talking*—and let that be it. The man who cannot simply walk along the street in the evening, savor the moment's coolness like everyone else does, and say, *That's it, that's all there is, this is simply this*, and go no further, not delve into what cannot be seen, not ask questions whose answers in the final analysis only he has any interest in . . . Now he understood—the distrust that other people showed for him was justified. For what was he to them if not a traitor, a man who considered himself (*knew* himself) to be above them, a man just waiting for the moment to laugh at them, a man who would not take seriously the things, which in their view justified their existence—the *other*, for them, the thing no one could see, the *useless?* He was a traitor. And, if he was to go on living, he had no alternative but always to be the outcast, the rejected, the scorned and despised. (*The Palace of the White Skunks* 144–145)

3. But if there was anything that stayed the same for him it was his fatal, inexplicable condition of being, then, the one whose was job it was to administer the screams. (My translation; I do not agree with Hurley's rendition; *Palace* 143)

4. Blasted old goats, what I'll never forgive them for is not that they brought me into the world but that they made me stay in it. (*Skunks* 31–32)

5. I can see us having tea, the two very close together, telling each other how our period often sharpens our senses and leads us from our ovaries to creation. Or, by contrast, distances us from it. How the blood leads new women to take us over, some of them movingly close to us; other, far away and terrible. This is because our menstrual blood contains the fierceness and the color of life, but also the germ of madness.

6. A VIOLET DANCE

Images of water and wide. Three people stare into space. They are sitting on a faded green sofa. Janosh, with his unbearably crooked now, straightens up; Morena, off of drugs, perches on the arm of the sofa and holds on to him. Genovesa walks up to the record player and turns the volume up. Patti Smith sings "Horses." Genovesa squats and follows the rhythm. Her dark skirt with yellow flowers flows against her hips. Johnny takes out a sharp pocket knife; with one movement, he slits his jugular. He falls slowly on the wet sands of the beach. A throng of horses moves towards him; deep red tongues of fire rise from their velvety snouts. There is a little place called space / The waves were coming in like radiant stallions / There's a little place called space / A promised land. Genovesa pulls herself up, arms akimbo, and takes her place next to Janosh. The thread of this story is accompanied by the dry hammering of metallic brushes. The three characters facing me look like the portrait of a deadly rock group. Time drifts by without clearing the pools of darkness in my mind. (*The Two Mujeres* 171)

7. The most positive result of all this was precisely the evidence that the foot represents for many people something that is at the same time very erotic and very unknown. As a consequence, I can say that I was enormously successful, to the extent that I awoke that sensibility in those few people who sought me and I provoked the mania in the head of many others who read my leaflet but who had neither the will or the guts to call me. Even if the majority of them never have anything to do with another man, they will probably be curious to try foot sex out with their girl friends or even their wives. This is very important, because the more people who get interested in the foot and the more the mystique takes hold, the better for me, since in may mean that I end up finding someone who thinks like I do.

8. As the reader will have noticed, stories like these were nothing more than a transposition of my real experiences onto a slightly more fantastic plane. This is something that now might seem to be somewhat superfluous, in view of this book where I am describing everything in exact terms.

9. In fact, what most bothered me was the abundance of books containing "memoirs" of the victims of repression that sought to denounce the violence they suffered but that, out of moral shame or ideological scruples, practiced self-censorship precisely when it came time to describing the scenes of torture, particularly ones involving implicit or explicit sexual acts, which end up being systematically omitted or euphemized.

10. Yes, because real torture, on my own hid—not on your life!

11. "Damn, this city sure has a lot of real crazies."

CHAPTER III. MARÍA ELENA WALSH

And now open your eyes real wide and brush the hair away from your ears, because what you are about to hear is absolutely marvelous. You'll never hear anything else like it in any other story.
Everybody take a good look around on this street, for a lot of things are happening but few of them are seen.

1. Walsh has written in her autobiographical statement, directed at her young readers: "Por otra parte, muchas personas que se dedicaron a escribir para chicos han sido solteros o sin hijos: Andersen, Gabriela Mistral, Lewis Carroll, José Sebastián Tallon, St. Exupéry . . . Crear para los chicos es quizás una manera de adoptarlos en general sin que a uno lo molesten en particular con sus travesuras. Una manera de ofrecerles—y pedirles—compañía y cariño" ("El cuento de la autora" 166–67).

2. Mrs. Crazy Thing runs, jumps and flys along the streets, calling for the doctor. But when she arrives her dog is dying with his tail sticking straight out and his belly

sunnyside up. / Mrs. Crazy Thing calls to firemen, the police and the tailor and the priest. But when they all get there, the little dog is happily dancing the rumba. / Mrs. Crazy Thing keeps on doing crazy things, her pants full of ants, while the little dog stays at home calmly smoking his pipe.

3. Mrs. Crazy Thing goes in search of a bug who lives high up, way high up, in a tree. The branch breaks and the naughty old lady lands smack-dab in a puddle. She lands right on her bottom in a puddle.

4. She doesn't know, she doesn't know, and she pushes a button to turn the moon on or to turn the sun off. / She listens with her tooth, she speaks with her ear, and she sweeps the sidewalk with a big spoon.

5. Mrs. Crazy Thing, with a nose made of meringue, "thet's gings wrong," I mean, always get things wrong.

6. The title is built on two names, both of which are eponyms: *chaucha* (feminine) is a young potato; *palito* (masculine) is a small stick.

7. Once upon a time there was a siren that lived in the River Paraná. She had a hut made of leaves on a floating island, and there she spent her days combing her long ebony hair and her nights singing, because it was her job to sing. (The river system of which the Paraná is a part is characterized by *camalotes,* floating clots of vegetation and debris.)

8. Even the animals who seemed among the worse, like the alligators and the snakes, approached her with affection.

9. That was all a long time ago. America was still in the hands of the Indians, and the Spaniards, with their beards and their ships, had not yet shown up.

10. I am a seafarer and an adventurer. I hail from Spain. Olé! I'm seeking glory, I'm seeking money, and I'll return heaped with both.

11. "Thank you, my friends, than you for this gift, for me the most beautiful one of all: liberty!

Dawn was breaking when the siren returned to her floating island, escorted through heaven and earth by all her friends. There in the distance the boat of the strange menwas floating away.

Alahí headed in the opposite direction with her floating island, downstream, to Paitití, the land of legends, where she still lives in freedom, always singing for those who know how to hear her.

12. One interesting aspect of Walsh's adult poetry is the troping of motifs from traditional children's poetry. This is especially evident in the collection *Juguemos en el mundo* (Let's Go Play in the Forest; 1970); cf., in particular, "¿Diablo estás?" (Devil, Are You There?; 28–29), which is built on the song "Juguemos en el bosque / mientras el lobo no está" (Let's go play in the forest / as long as the wolf is not there). Walsh's refrain becomes "Juguemos en el mundo / mientras el Diablo no está" (Let's go play in the forest / as long as the Devil's not there). Note also Walsh's ironic combination of the "adult" and "infantile" in her famous denunciation of the military dictatorship, in which she decries a tyrannical ideology that treats Argentine citizens as though they were irresponsible children: "Desventuras en el país-jardín-de-infantes" (Misadventures in the kindergarten country). It will also be recalled that Walsh sings her own composition "En el país de Nomeacuerdo" (In the Country of I Don't Remember) as a background motif to Luis Puenzo's highly

influential film *Historia oficial* (1985). The text is to be found in *El reino del revés* (The Upsidedown Country; 47).

13. I'm going to tell a story. One, two, three: Once upon a time. / How does it go after that?

14. The Marquis was bad and he took a stick and hit. . . . No, it wasn't the Marquis. I got it wrong. / It's not important. I'll go on. . . . / Then something happened which I can't remember very well. Maybe it happened on the train . . . And then. / I'm all lost.

15. I'd better stop right here. I think my mother's calling me too.

16. A Canary that barks is sad, and one that eats cardboard instead of birdseed, who travels by car and sunbathes at nights, does not, I'm almost certain, exist.

17. You may well ask me what one thing has to do with another.

18. You are the one who will end up changing the world.

CHAPTER IV. ARGENTINE JEWISH DRAMATISTS

1. JOHN.—That's it, historical. The story is not very funny if you tell it, but must have been irresistible to anyone seeing it. The kike looked at him with true error in his eyes. And Carlitos, all serious, with that seriousness of a dead drunk he had in those days, asked him "Are you Argentine?" Here, let me show you. I'm the kike, see? (*To the others.*) Now you'll see something marvelous. (*To the Bishop.*) You'll be Carlitos. (*John, taking the part of a character actor with true theatrical commitment, looks around for all of the necessary details to characterize the kike. He shoves a top hat down over his ears, he puts on a overcoat, and uses a napkin to simulate a beard.*)

2. But if for these reasons the reasons I have underscored could not diminish me, the accusation of being foreignizing, for a writer with a name like mine, presupposed a spiritual position, and perhaps a mental one, in opposition to that of a vast sector of society that endorsed the beautiful project of creating a national theater, one to which I aspired from my tenderest adolescence, awake or sleep, as a good craftsman. It was therefore natural that I would reject, intimately and profoundly, any such accusation.

In order to demonstrate this crass error, acts rather than words were necessary, and acts that were very clear. It was necessary for me to appeal to a world of things privately hidden, from the earliest years of my life, in that first period of spiritual formation in which, as luck would have it, the Argentine cityscape and the countryside alternated, brought together in an intrepid childhood.

3. Eichelbaum sought to criticize the system of capitalist exploitation on which agriculture in the Jewish colonies was based.

4. MYRIAM.—They went after me because of my condition as a Jew.

GASPAR.—That should have made you proud. And it should have made you understand my situation. We are, in reality, the Jews of today. We carry on our skin, as a permanent blemish, as an infamous scar, the sign of our race. You have become confused, you mix in, you fall apart, you change your names and even your religion. And the world accepts you and even receives you happily as a valuable catch.

NOTES

5. Concerning the importance of the IFT group, see Marial 142–46. Marial identifies the group with the subtitle Asociación Israelita Argentina Pro Arte. The IFT was responsible for introducing Argentine audiences to many important Jewish/Yiddish dramatists beginning in 1932–33.

6. DAVID.—(*He violently strips off the vestments and casts them aside, crying.*) Enough, Poppa!

SHOLEM.—(*Devastated, he doesn't move, without knowing what to do, mumbling out of defeat and humiliation.*) David! I am begging you please to stay.

DAVID.—I'm drowning, Poppa, I'm choking, I'm dying on the inside.

SHOLEM.—But you're killing me, David, you're destroying this house. Don't you see? (*He begins once again to act terrible and hard.*) Are you ashamed of me, of what you are?

7. What are you doing here? Put that cigarette out, you goy! It's already Friday night. You can't smoke. That would be the last straw, for Sholem to come in and find you smoking.

8. My story is that I am alive, and forever.

9. To a certain extent this theme of the struggle against the weight of past generations and ancestral history that pushes down on our consciousness, depriving it of the change and liberation of a full human being, is that of revolution, and it reappears in my way of seeing Lazarillo, of seeing him in the dual light of Spain and the Spanish-speaking community to which we as Latin Americans belong.

10. There is electroshock, a beating, a thousand and one nights of the shrieking of madmen that await me.

11. But I don't want to be a Jew—I just want to me a man, nothing more.

12. Cure me? Of what? I'm in a state of Grace. (*He caresses the Cross.*) What these people will never know is that I am a true knight of the Indies, and I will outlive them.

13. In all of José Rabinovich's books there is always the same vital force, the same life's suffering, the same overwhelming gray ruin of the unredeemable destiny of the poor, the same simplicity and the same intensity. What powerful forces would he be able to muster in the theater!

14. Mary, give me one or a dozen tranquilizers. The ones you give me have no effect. I need a powerful sedative. (*Very nervous.*) There is not a room in this house that does not turn into a rat run for me. I see one of my grandmothers at every turn, or one of my parents. Parents must think their sons and daughters stay children all their lives.

15. My God, that man has turned my entire house into a cemetery. Everywhere I step there is the smell of death. Jews forced pages of despair into the book of life. It's as though they could not exist without feeling themselves to be martyrs. If shadows did not exist, the Jews would have invented them.

16. See also Foster, "Matrimony and Religious Conflict: *El hijo del rabino*" (forthcoming) on Bernardo Gravier's 1932 play, perhaps the founding text in Argentina of interfaith matrimonial conflict.

17. The absurd without limits creates its own rules in Hebe Serebrisky.

18. The back room of a typical store in a provincial town where fabric, clothes, needles, and thread are sold. To the left, a curtain of faded blue velvet divides the back room from the front of the store. Except for this incongruous detail, the

decor of old furniture denotes a solid economic status. Stage right, there is another door that opens out directly on the street. An armchair. Hanging behind it is the enormous colorized photograph of the face of a child. To the right, a table with four chairs, a crystal cabinet with a mirror over it. In front of the armchair, a fancy one-piece stereo record player. Another door leads to the kitchen and the other rooms.

19. An orange light bathes the entire scene. A violin solo can be heard very softly. Don Elías is seated on a sort of throne which in reality is nothing more than his armchair on a raised platform in the form of a dice cup: a cylinder that is wider at the top than at the bottom and made of worked leather. Hugo is standing with his arms crossed in front of Don Elías. He is looking at him quizzically.

20. You shit of a kike!

21. Be patriotic, kill a Jew!

22. Our life is worth nothing more than a gob of spit.

23. In my opinion, the best thing you could do now is to get yourself a good death.

24. KRINSKY (*addressing the audience*).—Just get a look at her, would you!
LUBA (*addressing the audience*).—Just forget. . . . just forget. . . . Why remember?

25. They don't catch on to a thing because they don't understand Yiddish.

NOTES

⊷ References ⊶

CHAPTER I. SPANISH AMERICAN AND BRAZILIAN LITERATURE

I have listed here only those relatively scarce critical items that seek to incorporated Brazil within a globalized Latin American perspective.

Dixon, Paul B. *Reversible Readings; Ambiguity in Four Modern Latin American Narratives*. University: University of Alabama Press, 1985.

Fernández Moreno, César, general editor. *América Latina en su literatura*. México, D.F.: Siglo XXI, 1972.

Foster, David William. *Alternative Voices in the Contemporary Latin American Narrative*. Columbia: University of Missouri Press, 1985.

————. *Gay and Lesbian Themes in Latin American Literature*. Austin: University of Texas Press, 1991.

Foster, David William, ed. *Handbook of Latin American Literature*. 2d ed. New York: Garland, 1992.

Klein, Leonard S., ed. *Latin American Literature in the 20th Century: A Guide*. New York: Ungar, 1986.

Mac Adam, Alfred. *Modern Latin American Narratives: The Dreams of Reason*. Chicago: University of Chicago Press, 1977.

Peden, Margaret Sayers. *The Latin American Short Story: A Critical History*. Boston: Twayne, 1983.

Reis, Roberto, ed. *Toward Socio-Criticism: Selected Proceedings of the Conference "Luso-Brazilian Literatures: A Socio-Critical Approach*. Tempe: Center for Latin American Studies, Arizona State University, 1991.

Rodríguez Monegal, Emir. *Narradores de esta América*. Montevideo: Alfa, 1969–; Buenos Aires: Alfa Argentina, 1974.

Santiago, Silviana. *Uma literatura nos trópicos*. São Paulo: Perspectiva, 1978.

CHAPTER II. SOME PROPOSALS

Acevedo, Zelmar. *Homosexualidad: hacia la destrucción de los mitos*. Buenos Aires: Ediciones del Ser, 1985.

165

Araujo, Denize Correa. "The Spheres of Power in *Xica da Silva.*" *Rocky Mountain Review* 46, nos. 1–2 (1992): 37–43.

Arenas, Reinaldo. *The Palace of the White Skunks.* Translated by Andrew Hurley. New York: Viking, 1990.

————. *El palacio de las blanquísimas mofetas.* Carcas: Monte Avila, 1980.

"Arenas's Last Words." *New York Review of Books* 38, no. 12 (27 June 1991): 65.

Argüelles, Lourdes, and B. Ruby Rich. "Homosexuality, Homophobia, and Revolution: Notes Toward an Understanding of the Cuban Lesbian and Gay Male Experience." *Signs* 9, no. 4 (1984): 683–99; 11, no. 1 (1985): 120–36.

Bautista, Juan Carlos. "La sonrisa de Sor Juana." *Fem* 14, no. 95 (1990): 13–16.

Bergman, David. *Gaiety Transfigured; Gay Self-Representation in American Literature.* Madison: University of Wisconsin Press, 1991.

Blanco, José Joaquín. *Función de medianoche.* 1981. Reprint. México, D.F.: Era/ SEP Cultura, 1986.

————. *La paja en el ojo; ensayos de crítica.* Puebla, Méx.: ICUAP, Centro de Estudios Contemporáneos, Editorial Universidad Autónoma de Puebla, 1980.

Bronski, Michael. *Culture Clash: The Making of Gay Sensibility.* Boston: South End Press, 1984.

Bruce-Novoa, Juan. "Homosexuality and the Chicano Novel." *Confluencia; revista hispánica de cultura y literatura* 2, no. 1 (1986): 69–77. Also 98–106 in *European Perspectives on Hispanic Literature of the United States.* Edited by Genvieve Fabre. Houston: Arte Público Press, 1988.

Cabrera Infante, Guillermo. "Reinaldo Arena o la destrucción del sexo." *El País* [Madrid], 1 June 1992, pp. 7–8.

Califia, Pat. *Macho sluts; erotic fiction.* Boston: Alyson, 1988.

Cohen, Ed. "Foucauldian Necrologies: 'Gay' 'Politics'? 'Politically Gay'?" *Textual Practices* 2, no. 1 (1988): 87–101.

differences; a Journal of Feminist Cultural Studies 3, no. 2 (Summer 1991). Special issue: Queer Theory: Lesbian and Gay Sexualities.

Dollimore, Jonathan. *Sexual Dissidence; Augustine to Wilde, Freud to Foucault.* Oxford: Clarendon Press, 1991.

Dworkin, Andrea. *Intercourse.* New York: Free Press, 1987.

Faderman, Lillian. *Odd Girls and Twilight Lovers; a History of Lesbian Life in Twentieth-Century America.* New York: Columbia University Press, 1991.

Felski, Rita. *Beyond Feminist Aesthetics; Feminist Literature and Social Change.* Cambridge: Harvard University Press, 1989.

Foster, David William. *Alternate Voices in the Contemporary Latin American Narrative.* Columbia: University of Missouri Press, 1985.

————. *Contemporary Argentine Cinema.* Columbia: University of Missouri Press, 1992.

————. *From Mafalda to Los supermachos: Latin American Graphic Humor.* Boulder, Colo.: Lynn Rienner, 1989.

————. *Gay and Lesbian Themes in Latin American Literature.* Austin: University of Texas Press, 1991.

————. "Narrativa testimonial argentina durante los años del proceso." In *Testimonio y literatura,* edited by René Jara and Hernán Vidal, 138–54.

Minneapolis: Institute for the Study of Ideologies and Literature, 1986.

———. "Los parámetros de la narrativa argentina durante el 'Proceso de Reorganización Nacional.'" In *Ficción y política; la narrativa argentina durante el proceso militar.* 98–108. Buenos Aires: Alianza Editorial; Minneapolis: Institute for the Study of Ideologies and Literature, 1987.

———. Review of *Adonis García: A Picaresque Novel* by Luis Zapata. In *My Deep Dark Pain is Love: A Collection of Latin American Gay Fiction. Chasqui* 13, no. 1 (November 1983): 90–92.

———. "The Roots of Literary Tradition: Popular Culture." Forthcoming, p. 8–9.

———. "The Search for Text: Some Examples of Latin American Gay Writing." *Ibero-Amerikanisches Archiv,* neue folge 14, no. 3 (1988): 329–56.

Foster, Stephen Wayne. "Latin American Studies." *Cabirion and Gay Books Bulletin* 11 (1984): 2–7, 29.

Franco, Jean. *Plotting Women: Gender and Representation in Mexico.* New York: Columbia University Press, 1989.

Foucault, Michel. *The History of Sexuality.* Translated by A. M. Sheridan Smith. New York: Vintage Books, 1980.

Fry, Peter. "Da hierarquia à igualdade: a construção histórica da homosexualidade." In *Para inglês ver; identidade e política na cultura brasileira.* 87–115. Rio de Janeiro: Zahar, 1982.

———. "Léonie, Pompinha, Amaro e Aleixo, prostituição, homosexualidade e raça em dois romances naturalistas." In *Caminhos cruzados; linguagem, antropologia, ciências naturais.* 33–51. São Paulo: Brasiliense, 1982.

Fuss, Diane. *Inside/Out: Lesbian Theories, Gay Theories.* New York: Routledge, 1991.

García Canclini, Néstor. *Arte popular y sociedad en América Latina; teorías estéticas y ensayos de transformación.* México, D.F.: Grijalbo, 1977.

———. *Las culturas populares en el capitalismo.* La Habana: Casa de las Américas, 1982.

Gilbert, Sandra. "Life's Empty Pack: Notes toward a Literary Daughteronomy." *Critical Inquiry* 11, no. 3 (1985): 355–84.

Greenberg, David F. *The Construction of Homosexuality.* Chicago: University Press, 1988.

Gregorich, Luis. *Literatura y homosexualidad y otros ensayos.* Buenos Aires: Editorial Legasa, 1985.

Homosexuality: Power & Politics. Edited by Gay Left Collective. London: Allison and Busby, 1980.

Howes, Robert. "The Literature of Outsiders: The Literature of the Gay Community in Latin America." In *Latin American Masses and Minorities: Their Images and Realities,* edited by Dan C. Hazen, 1:288–304, 580–91. Madison: SALALM Secretariat, Memorial Library, University of Wisconsin, 1985.

Jameson, Fredric. *Postmodernism, or the Cultural Logic of Latin Capitalism.* Durham, N.C.: Duke University Press, 1990.

Jáuregui, Carlos Luis. *La homosexualidad en la Argentina.* Buenos Aires: Ediciones Tarso, 1978.

Jockl, Alejandro. *Ahora, los gay.* Buenos Aires: Ediciones de la Pluma, 1984.

Levi Calderón, Sara. *Dos mujeres*. México, D.F.: Editorial Diana, 1990.
———. *The Two Mujeres*. Translated by Gina Kaufer. San Francisco: Aunt Lute Books, 1991.
Leyland, Winston. *My Deep Dark Pain is Love; a Collection of Latin American Gay Fiction*. San Francisco: Gay Sunshine Press, 1983.
Leyland, Winston, ed. *Now the Volcano; an Anthology of Latin American Gay Literature*. Translated by Erskine Lane, Franklin D. Blanton, and Simon Karlinsky. San Francisco: Gay Sunshine Press, 1979.
Lima, Délcio Monteiro de. *Os homoeróticos*. Rio de Janeiro: Francisco Alves, 1983.
Mattoso, Glauco. *Dicionarinho do palavrão & correlatos, inglês-português, português-inglês*. 2d ed. Rio de Janeiro: Editora Record, 1991.
———. *Manual do pedólatra amador: aventuras & leituras de um tarado por pés*. Prefácio, Leo Gilson Ribeiro; posfácio, Néstor Perlongher. São Paulo: Editora Expressão, 1986.
Mattoso, Glauco, and Marcatti. *As aventuras de Glaucomix o pedólatra*. São Paulo: Quadrinhos Abriu; Quadrinhos Fechou, 1990.
Míccolis, Leila, and Herbert Daniel. *Jacarés e lobisomens: dois ensaios sobre a homosexualidade*. Rio de Janeiro: Achiamé, 1983.
Monsiváis, Carlos. *Amor perdido*. México, D.F.: Era, 1977.
———. *Días de guardar*. 4th ed. México, D.F.: Era, 1971.
———. *Escenas de pudor y liviandad*. 9th ed. México, D.F.: Grijalbo, 1988.
Mott, Luiz. *Escravidão, homosexualidade e demonologia*. São Paulo: Icone, 1988.
Murray, Stephen O., ed. *Male Homosexuality in Central and South America*. San Francisco: Instituto Obregón; New York: GAU-NY, 1987.
Parker, Richard G. *Bodies, Pleasures, and Passions; Sexual Culture in Contemporary Brazil*. Boston: Beacon Press, 1990.
Paz, Octavio. *Sor Juana Inés de la Cruz o las trampas de la fe*. México, D.F.: Fondo de Cultura Económica, 1982.
Pérez, Emma. "Sexuality and Discourse: Notes from a Chicana Survivor." In *Chicana Lesbians: The Girls Our Mothers Warned Us about*. 159–84. San Francisco: Aunt Lute Books, 1991.
Perlongher, Néstor Osvaldo. *O negócio do michê: prostituição viril em São Paulo*. São Paulo: Editora Brasiliense, 1987.
Políticas culturales en América Latina. Edited by Néstor García Cancilini. México, D.F.: Grijalbo, 1987.
Puig, Manuel. "El error gay." *El porteño*, September 1990, pp. 32–33.
Rechy, John. *Rushes; a Novel*. New York: Grove Press, 1979.
Reinhardt, Karl J. "The Image of Gays in Chicano Prose Fiction." *Explorations in Ethnic Studies* 4, no. 2 (1981): 41–55.
Rich, Adrienne. "Compulsory Heterosexuality and Lesbian Existence." In *Blood, Bread, and Poetry; Selected Prose 1979–1985*. 23–75. New York: W. W. Norton, 1986.
Roffiel, Rosamaría. *Amora*. México, D.F.: Editorial Planeta Mexicana, 1989.
Roof, Judith. *A Lure of Knowledge: Lesbian Sexuality and Theory*. New York: Columbia University Press, 1991.
Schaefer-Rodríguez, Claudia. "The Power of Subversive Imagination: Homosexual

Utopian Discourse in Contemporary Mexican Literature." *Latin American Literary Review* 33 (1989): 29–41.

Schneider, Luis Mario. "El tema homosexual en la nueva narrativa mexicana." *Casa del tiempo* [Mexico] 49–50 (1985): 82–86.

Schwartz, Kessel. "Homosexuality as a Theme in Representative Contemporary Spanish American Novels." *Kentucky Romance Quarterly* 22 (1975): 247–57.

Sedgwick, Eve Kosofsky. *Epistemology of the Closet.* Berkeley and Los Angeles: University of California Press, 1991.

Shaw, Donald A. "Notes on the Presentation of Sexuality in the Modern Spanish-American Novel." *Bulletin of Hispanic Studies* 59 (1982): 275–82.

Soto, Francisco. "Reinaldo Arena's Literary Legacy." *Christopher Street* 156 (1991): 12–16.

Spivak, Gayatri Chakravorty. "Can the Subaltern Speak?" In *Marxism and the Interpretation of Culture,* edited by Cary Nelson and Lawrence Grossberg, 271–313. Urbana: University of Illinois Press, 1988.

Suleiman, Susan Rubin. "The Politics and Poetics of Female Eroticism." In *Subversive Intent; Gender, Politics, and the Avant-Garde.* 118–40. Cambridge: Harvard University Press, 1990.

Theweleit, Kalus. *Male Fantasies.* Minneapolis: University of Minnesota Press, 1987–89.

Trevisan, João S. *Perverts in Paradise.* Translated by Martin Foreman. London: GMP Publications, 1986. Originally published as *Devassos no paraíso* (1986).

Vidal, Gore. *The City and the Pillar Revised.* New York: E. P. Dutton, 1965.

Villanueva, Alfredo. "Machismo vs. Gayness: Latin American Fiction." *Gay Sunshine* 29–30 (1976): 22.

Whitam, Frederick L., and Robin M. Mathy. *Male Homosexuality in Four Societies: Brazil, Guatemala, the Philippines, and the United States.* New York: Praeger, 1985.

Yingling, Thomas E. *Hart Crane and the Homosexual Text: New Thresholds, New Anatomies.* Chicago: University of Chicago Press, 1990.

Young, Allen. *Gays under the Cuban Revolution.* San Francisco: Grey Fox Press, 1981.

Zimmerman, Bonnie. *The Safe Sea of Women: Lesbian Fiction, 1969–1989.* Boston: Beacon Press, 1990.

CHAPTER III. MARÍA ELENA WALSH

"El cuento infantil no entra en el Parnaso." *Puro cuento* 2, no. 7 (1987): 1–6, 56.

Dorfman, Ariel. *The Empire's Old Clothes: What the Long Ranger, Babar, and Other Innocent Heroes Do to Our Minds.* New York: Pantheon Books, 1983.

Dorfman, Ariel, and Armand Mattelart. *Para leer al Pato Donald.* 5th ed. Buenos Aires: Siglo XXI, 1973.

Dujovne, Alicia. *María Elena Walsh*. Madrid: Ediciones Júcar, 1982.

Felski, Rita. *Beyond Feminist Aesthetics; Feminist Literature and Social Change.* Cambridge: Harvard University Press, 1989.

Foster, David William. "Playful Ecphrasis: María Elena Walsh and Children's Literature in Argentina." *Mester* 13, no. 1 (1984): 40–51.

Gallelli, Graciela Rosa. *Panorama de la literatura infantil-juvenil argentina; guía comentada de los últimos 30 años a partir de 1950.* Buenos Aires: Editorial Plus Ultra, 1985.

Hunt, Peter. *Criticism, Theory, and Children's Literature.* Oxford: Basil Blackwell, 1991.

Lurie, Alison. *Don't Tell the Grown-ups: Subversive Children's Literature.* Boston: Little, Brown, 1990.

Pagni, Andrea. "María Elena Walsh und die Alltagslyric in Buenos Aires." In *Die Legitimation der Alltagssprache in der modernen Lyrik: Antworten aus Europa und Lateinamerika,* edited by Harold Wentzlaff-Eggebert, 165–84. Erlangen: Universitätsbund Erlangen-Nürnberg, 1984.

Pastoriza de Etchebarne, Dora. *El cuento en la literatura infantil; ensayo crítico.* Buenos Aires: Editorial Kapelusz, 1962.

Phillips, Jerry, and Ian Wojcik-Andrews. "Notes toward a Marxist Critical Practice." *Children's Literature* 18 (1990): 127–30.

Sánchez Lihón, Danilo. "Rebelión y soledad: reflexiones sobre literatura infantil." *Tierra nuestra* 1, no. 1 (1991): 43–52.

Walsh, María Elena. *Chaucha y palito.* Buenos Aires: Editorial Sudamericana, 1977.

———. "El cuento de la autora." In Walsh, *Chaucha y palito.* 149–69.

———. *Cuentopos de Gulubú.* Buenos Aires: Editorial Sudamericana, 1969.

———. "Desventuras en el país-jardín-de-infantes." *Clarín,* 16 August, 1979, "Cultura y nación" suppl., p. 4. The headline reads, "La censura y sus perjuicios en nuestra cultura."

———. *Juguemos en el mundo.* Buenos Aires: Editorial Sudamericana, 1970.

———. *Palomita de la puna.* Buenos Aires: Editorial Sudamericana, 1987.

———. *Los poemas.* Buenos Aires: Editorial Sudamericana, 1984.

———. *El reino del revés.* Buenos Aires: Luis Fariña Editor, 1963.

———. *La sirena y el capitán.* 1974. Reprint. Buenos Aires: Ángel Estrada, 1977.

———. *Tutú Marambá.* Buenos Aires: Editorial Sudamericana, 1969.

———. *Zoo loco.* Buenos Aires: Editorial Sudamericana, 1970.

CHAPTER IV. ARGENTINE JEWISH DRAMATISTS

Aínsa, Fernando. "La Tierra Prometida como motivo en la narrativa argentina." *Hispamérica* 53–54 (1989): 3–23.

Blanco Amores de Pagella, Angela. *Motivaciones del teatro argentino en el teatro argentino en el siglo XX.* Buenos Aires: Ediciones Culturales Argentinas, 1983.

Bristow, Edward J. *Prostitution and Prejudice; the Jewish Fight against White Slavery 1870–1939.* Oxford: Clarendon Press, 1982.

REFERENCES

Cruz, Jorge. *Samuel Eichelbaum.* Buenos Aires: Ediciones Culturales Argentinas, 1962.

Diament, Mario. *Conversaciones con un judío [Mario Diament interviews Máximo Yagupsky].* Buenos Aires: Timerman Editores, 1977.

Eichelbaum, Samuel. "El judío Aaron." *Talía* 32 (1967): suppl.

———. *Nadie la conoció nunca.* In Eichelbaum, *Tejido de madre. Nadie la conoció nunca.* 41–62. Buenos Aires: Argentores, Ediciones del Carro de Tespis, 1956.

Elkin, Judith Laikin. "A Demographic Profile of Latin American Jewry." *American Jewish Archives* 34 (1982): 231–48.

———. *Jews of the Latin American Republics.* Chapel Hill: University of North Carolina Press, 1980.

Foster, David William. *The Argentine Teatro Independiente.* York, S.C.: Spanish Literature Publications, 1986.

———. "Estrategias narrativas en *Las historias para ser contadas* de Osvaldo Dragún." *Anales de literatura hispánica* 7 (1978): 131–40.

———. "Ideological Shift in the Rural Images in Florencio Sánchez's Theater." *Hispanic Journal* 11, no. 1 (1990): 97–106.

———. "Matrimony and Religious Conflict: *El hijo del rabino.*" In *Tradition and Innovation,* edited by Robert Di Antonio and Nora Glickmann, Albany: State University of New York Press, forthcoming.

Foster, David William, and Naomi Lindstrom. "Jewish Argentine Authors: A Registry." *Revista interamericana de bibliografía* 41, no. 3 (1991): 478–503; 41, no. 4 (1991): 655–82.

Gambaro, Griselda. *Teatro: Nada que ver. Sucede lo que pasa.* Ottawa: Girol Books, 1983.

García, Germán. *El inmigrante en la novela argentina.* Buenos Aires: Hachette, 1970.

Glickman, Nora. "The Jewish White Slave Trade in Latin American Writings." *American Jewish Archives* 34 (1982): 178–89.

Goldenberg, Jorge. *Krinsky.* Buenos Aires: Ediciones de Arte Gaglianone, 1984.

———. *Relevo 1923.* La Habana: Casa de las Américas, 1975.

Goodman, Robert Alan. "The Image of the Jew in Argentine Literature as Seen by Argentine Jewish Writers." New York University, 1972.

Halac, Ricardo. "El teatro de Germán Rozenmacher y la tensión entre el judaísmo y la revolución." *Los libros* 23 (1971): 24–25.

Karavellos, Panos D. *La dramaturgia de Samuel Eichelbaum.* Montevideo: Geminis, 1976.

Kleiner, Alberto. *La temática judía en el teatro argentino.* Buenos Aires: Libreros y Editores del Polígano, 1983. Contains: Luis Karduner, "Misión del escritor judío en la literatura argentina," 17–21; and Lázaro Schallman, "La temática judía en el teatro argentino," 25–56.

Liebman, Seymour B. "Argentine Jews and Their Institutions," *Jewish Social Studies* 43 (1981): 311–28.

Lindstrom, Naomi. *Argentine-Jewish Writers.* Columbia: University of Missouri Press, 1989.

REFERENCES

————. "Problems and Possibilities in the Analysis of Jewish Argentine Literary Works." *Latin American Research Review* 18, no. 1 (1983): 118–26.

Lipski, John M. *Linguistic Aspects of Spanish-English Language Switching.* Tempe: Center for Latin American Studies, Arizona State University, 1985.

Marial, José. *El teatro independiente.* Buenos Aires: Alpe, 1955.

McGrady, Donald. "Social Irony in *Lazarillo de Tormes* and Its Implications for Authorship." *Romance Philology* 23 (1969–70): 557–67.

Navarro Gerassi, Marysa. *Los nacionalistas,* translated by Alberto Ciria. Buenos Aires: Editorial Jorge Alvarez, 1968.

Neglia, Erminio G. *Aspectos del teatro moderno hispanoamericano.* Bogotá: Editorial Stella, 1975.

————. *Pirandello y la dramática rioplatense.* Firenze: Valmartina Editore, 1970.

Rabinovich, José. *Con pecado concebida.* Buenos Aires: Ediciones del Carro de Tespis, 1975.

————. *Sobras de juventud; memorias.* Buenos Aires: Ediciones Crisol, 1976.

Rozenmacher, Germán. *El Lazarillo de Tormes.* Buenos Aires: Talía, 1971.

————. *Réquiem para un viernes a la noche; drama en un réquiem y un acto.* Buenos Aires: Talía, 1964.

————. *Simón Brumelstein, el caballero de Indias.* Buenos Aires: Argentores, 1987.

Sadow, Stephen A. "*Judíos y gauchos*: The Search for Identity in Argentine-Jewish Literature." *American Jewish Archives* 34 (1982): 164–77.

Sánchez Sívori, Amalia. "La inmigración y la literatura argentina." In *Inmigración y nacionalidad.* 93–143. Buenos Aires: Paidós, 1967.

Sandrow, Nahma. *Vagabond Stars; a World History of Yiddish Theater.* New York: Harper & Row, 1977.

Schallman, Lázaro. "El judaísmo y los judíos a través de las letras argentinas." *Comentario* 48 (1966): 113–24.

Schwartz, Kessel. "The Jew in Argentine Literature." *American Hispanist* 19 (1977): 9–12.

Sebreli, Juan José. *La cuestión judía en la Argentina.* Buenos Aires: Tiempo Contemporáneo, 1968.

Senkman, Leonardo. *La identidad judía en la literatura argentina.* Buenos Aires: Editorial Pardes, 1983.

Serebrisky, Hebe. *Teatro.* Buenos Aires: Ediciones Scena, 1982.

Sofer, Eugene E. *From Pale to Pampa, a Social History of the Jews of Buenos Aires.* New York: Holmes & Meier, 1982.

Sosnowski, Saúl. "Contemporary Jewish-Argentine Writers: Tradition and Politics." *Latin American Literary Review* 12 (1982): 1–14.

————. "Germán Rozenmacher: tradiciones, rupturas y desencuentros." *Revista de crítica literaria latinoamericana* 6 (1977): 93–110.

————. "Latin American Jewish Writers: a Bridge toward History." *Prooftexts* 4 (1984): 71–92.

————. *La orilla inminente; escritores judíos argentinos.* Buenos Aires: Editorial Legasa, 1987.

Tiempo, César. *El teatro soy yo; farsa dramática en tres actos.* Buenos Aires: Librerías Anaconda, 1933.

REFERENCES

———. "Treinta preguntas a José Rabinovich, un narrador de la estirpe de Agnon." *Davar* 115 (1967): 61–78.

Timerman, Jacobo. *Prisoner without a Name, Cell without a Number,* translated by Toby Talbot. New York: Knopf/Random House, 1981. Orig. *Preso sin nombre, celda sinnúmero.* Buenos Aires: El Cid Editor, 1982.

Tirri, Néstor. *Realismo y teatro argentino.* Buenos Aires: La Bastilla, 1973.

Viñas, David. *En la semana trágica.* Buenos Aires: Editorial Jorge Alvarez, 1966.

Weisbrot, Robert. *The Jews of Argentina, from the Inquisition to Perón.* Philadelphia: Jewish Publication Society of America, 1979.

Woodyard, George. "The Theatre of the Absurd in Spanish America." *Comparative Drama* 3, no. 3 (1969): 183–92.

"Yiddish Theater in Argentina." In *Cinco años de vida comunitaria judía, 1958–1962.* 522–32. Buenos Aires: Asociación Mutual Israelita Argentina, 1963.

Zago, Mauricio. *Pioneros de la Argentina, los inmigrantes judíos; Pioneers in Argentina, the Jewish immigrants.* Buenos Aires: Manrique Zago Ediciones, 1982.

Zayas de Lima, Perla. *Diccionario de autores teatrales argentinos (1950–1980).* Buenos Aires: Editorial Rodolfo Alonso, 1981.

INDEX

Acevedo, Juan: *Cuy*, 35
Aguinis, Marcos, 147
Agustini, Delmira, 17
Alegría, Fernando, 77
Alfonsín, Raúl, 96
Almendros, Néstor, 44; *Conducta impropia*, 30, 44
Almodóvar, Pedro, 32
Amado, Jorge, 4, 10, 31; *Doña Flor e seus dois maridos* (*Dona Flor and Her Two Husbands*), 31
Andrade, Mário de, 3; *Macunaíma*, 8
Arenas, Reinaldo, 30, 41, 48, 70; *Arturo, la estrella más brillante*, 30, 44, 48; *El mundo alucinante*, 45; *El palacio de las blanquísimas mofetas*, 45–49; *Vieja Rosa*, 45
Arévalo Martínez, José: "El hombre que parecía un caballo," 22
Arguedas, José María, 14
Arlt, Roberto, 21, 103; *El juguete rabioso*, 21
Azevedo, Aluísio: *O cortiço*, 50

B'nai B'rith Anti-Defamation League, 96
Babenco, Héctor, 19, 28
Barbachano Ponce, Manuel: *El diario de José Toledo*, 50
Barletta, Leónidas, 103
Blanco, José Joaquín, 21, 22

Bombal, María Luisa, 16
Boom, Latin American fiction, 9
Borges, Jorge Luis, 7, 9, 107
Bradbury, Ray, 77
Braga, Sônia, 31
Brandão, Ignácio Luis, 20, 21; *Não verás país nenhum* (*And Still the Earth*), 20
Brazil (film), 20
Brunet, Marta, 16
Bueno, Ruth, 21
Bullrich, Silvina, 18
Bund Movement, 105
Burroughs, William S., 43, 48; *Queer*, 43
Butor, Michel, 77

Califa, Pat: *Macho Sluts*, 66
Calva, José Rafael: *Utopía gay*, 42
Caminha, Adolfo, 21, 50; *Bom Crioulo*, 21, 50, 53
Carneiro, André, 21
Carnival, 31
Carpentier, Alejo, 9
Castellanos, Rosario, 18
Castro, Fidel, 29, 30
Cavani, Liliana: *The Night Porter*, 67
Cervantes Saavedra, Miguel de: *Don Quixote*, 107
Children's literature, 73, 74
Chocrón, Isaac, 21

Cohen, Ed, 69
Cortázar, Julio, 10, 11
Cossa, Roberto, 139

D'Halmar, Augusto: La pasión y muerte del cura Deusto, 21
Década Infame, 114
Derrida, Jacques, 89
DiAntonio, Robert, xi
Diegues, Carlos, 31; Xica da Silva, 31, 32
Disney, Walt, 75, 80
Dollimore, Jonathan, 57
Donald Duck, 75
Donoso, José: El lugar sin límites, 44
Dorfman, Ariel: The Empire's Old Clothes, 93
Dr. Seuss, 78
Dragún, Osvaldo, 98, 125, 139; Historias para ser contadas, 125
Durcal, Rocío, 36
Dworkin, Andrea, 66

Eco, Umberto, 77
Ecofeminism, 88
Eichelbaum, Samuel, 98–109, 133, 138, 147, 153; Un guapo de 900, 104, 110; El judío Aaron, 104–10, 133, 148; Nadie la conoció nunca, 98–102, 147; Un tal Severando Gómez, 104, 110

Feierstein, Ricardo, 147
Feminine/feminist écriture, 89, 92, 152
Feminism, 15, 89, 92, 153
Feminist criticism, vii, 16–19
Ferré, Rosario, 17, 18
Fonseca, Rubem, 21
Foucault, Michel, 42, 43, 55, 58, 69
Fry, Peter, 70; Para inglês ver, 70
Fuentes, Carlos, 9
Fuertes, Gloria, 93

Gabriel, Juan, 36, 37
Gambaro, Griselda, 17, 18, 77, 93, 137, 138, 139; El campo, 138; El desatino, 138; Los siameses, 138

Gamboa, Federico: Santa, 51
García Márquez, Gabriel, 33, 88; Cien años de soledad, 88
Gerchunoff, Alberto: Los gauchos judíos, 107, 109
Glickmann, Nora, xi
Goldenberg, Jorge, 143–47; Krinsky, 143–47; Relevo 1923, 143
Golding, William: Lord of the Flies, 78
Goloboff, Gerardo Mario, 147
Gorostiza, Carlos, 139
Gorriti, Juana Manuela, 16
Graiver, Bernardo: El hijo del rabino, 136
Guillén, Nicolás, 5
Güiraldes, Ricardo: Don Segundo Sombra, 8

Halac, Ricardo, 98, 127, 139
Hall, Radclyffe: The Well of Loneliness, 56
Hannois, Amelia, 77
Heifitz, Yasha, 140
Highbridge, Patricia: Price of Salt, 56
Homosexuality, 22, 23

Ibarbourou, Juana de, 135
Ibsen, Henrik: An Enemy of the People, 108; Ghosts, 108; The Wild Duck, 108
Ionesco, Eugène, 77

James, Henry: The Bostonians, 43
Jameson, Fredric, 50
Jewish identity, viii, xi, 97, 110, 118, 122, 136, 143
Johnson, Virginia E., 60
Jorge, Miguel, 19
The Joys of Gay Sex, 58
Juana Inés de la Cruz, 52

Kaufer, Gina, 52
Kramer, Larry, 43, 46; Faggots, 43

Latin American Report, 96
Lesbian and Gay Writing, vii, x, 21–24, 25–71, 152

Levi Calderón, Sara, 50–57, 70, 153;
Dos mujeres, 50–57
Lindstrom, Naomi, xi, 96, 98
Lispector, Clarice, 15, 16, 19, 77
Louzeiro, José: Aracelli, meu amor,
19; Lúcio Flávio, o passageiro da
agonia, 19
Lurie, Alison: Don't Tell the Grown-
ups: Subversive Children's Litera-
ture, 79
Lynch, Marta, 17, 18; Informe bajo
llave, 17; La penúltima versión de la
Colorada Villanueva, 17

Machado de Assis, Joaquim Maria 3,
15
Marchant Lazcano, Jorge, 21
Marx, Harpo, 144, 147
Masters, William E., 60
Mastretta, Angeles, 51, 52; Arráncame
la vida, 51
Matto de Turner, Clorinda, 16
Mattoso, Glauco, 61–70, 155; Boca
do inferno Vol. 1. Manual do pedó-
latra amador; aventuras & leituras
de um tratado por pés (Manual of
the Amateur Foot Lover; Adven-
tures and Readings of Someone Wild
for Feet), 61–70. (Comic book ver-
sion: As aventuras de Glaucomix o
pedólatra).
Melville, Herman: Billy Budd, 43
Mendoza, María Luisa: De ausencia,
18
Meyer, Rabbi Marshall, 96
Modernism, 8, 9
Modernism (Brazil), 3–8
Modernism (Spanish America), 5, 6
Monsiváis, Carlos, 36, 51
Monti, Ricardo, 139
Mother Goose, 80

Nalé Roxlo, Conrado, 103
Neruda, Pablo, 5, 7, 33
Nervo, Amado, 51
New Criticism, 81, 89
Noll, José Gilberto, 21

Novo, Salvador, 51

Ocampo, Silvina, 77

Parker, Richard G., 60
Pavlovsky, Eduardo, 139
Paz, Octavio, 52
Pellegrini, Carlos, 108
Perlongher, Néstor, 69
Perón, Juan Domingo, 108, 114, 118
Peyrú, Graciela M., 138
Pirandello, Luigi, 116, 117
Pizarnik, Alejandra, 93, 153
Poniatowska, Elena, 17–19; Hasta no
verte Jesus mío, 19; La noche de
Tlatelolco, 19
Pornochanchada, 32
Postcolonial criticism, 151, 153
Postmodernism, 5, 62
Potter, Beatrix, 78, 80
Puenzo, Luis: La historia oficial, 152
Puig, Manuel, 22, 28, 42, 154, 155; El
beso de la mujer araña, 24, 28, 43
Puro cuento, 93

Queer Theory, 49

Rabinovich, José, 132–38, 148; Con
pecado concebida, 132–37, 148; El
gran castigo, 132, 136; Sobras de
juventud, 132; Tercera clase, 135
Raznovich, Diana, 98
Rechy, John, 51, 52, 66; Rushes, 66;
City of Night, 51
Rich, Adrienne, 54
Rinaldi, Susana, 36
Roa Bastos, Augusto, 14, 77
Rodríguez, Jesusa, 52
Roffiel, Rosamaría, 50–52; Amora,
50–52
Rosa, João Guimarães, 3, 9, 10, 12–15
Rozenmacher, Germán, 119–32, 138,
148, 153; El Lazarillo de Tormes,
125–28; Réquiem para un viernes
a la noche, 119–25; Simón Brumel-
stein, el caballero de Indias, 128–31
Rulfo, Juan, 9, 12–15

Sánchez, Florencio, 107, 108, 118; *La gringa*, 107, 108
Sarduy, Severo, 14
Science fiction, 19, 20
Segovia, Pedro: *Tango argentino*, 38
La Semana Trágica, 100, 101
Sendak, Maurice: *Where the Wild Things Are*, 78
Senkman, Leonardo, 96, 104, 117
Serebrisky, Hebe, 137–39, 148, 153; *Don Elías campeón*, 139–43
Silva, Aguinaldo: *No país das sombras*, 22–24
Silverstein, Shel: *Where the Sidewalk Ends*, 78
Somigliana, Carlos, 139
Sosnowski, Saúl, 96, 119
Steimberg, Alicia, 147, 153
Stevenson, Robert Luis: *Dr. Jekyll and Mr. Hyde*, 43
Subaltern studies, 151

Tango, 38–40
Teatro Independiente, 97, 103, 110, 115, 148
Telles, Lygia Fagundes, 16
Theater of the Absurd, 137
Tiempo, César (pseudo. Israel Zeitlin), 103, 110–18, 133, 138, 148, 153; *Pan criollo*, 111–13, 133, 136; *El teatro soy yo*, 113–18, 148
Timerman, Jacobo, 96
Torres Bodet, Jaime, 51

Vallejo, César, 5, 7
Vanguardismo, 5, 7
Vargas Llosa, Mario, 9, 29
Verbitsky, Bernardo, 132
Vidal, Gore, 42, 43; *The City and the Pillar*, 42
Villaurrutia, Xavier, 51
Villordo, Oscar Hermes, 21, 22
Viñas, David, 29; *En la semana trágica*, 145

Walsh, María Elena, xi, 73–94, 152; *Cancionero contra el mal de ojo*, 92; *Chaucha y palito*, 73, 85; *Cuentopos de Gulubú*, 91; "Desastres," 83, 84; "Doña Disparate," 83, 84; "El perrito loquito," 82, 84; *El reino del revés*, 73, 90, 93; *La sirena y el capitán*, 86–88; *Tutú Marambá*, 81; "Voy a contar un cuento," 90; *Zoo loco*, 92, 93
Westheimer, Dr. Ruth, 60
Whitman, Walt: *Leaves of Grass*, 43
Wilde, Oscar: *Picture of Dorian Gray*, 43
Winston, Leyland, 21

Zapata, Luis, 21, 22, 51–53; *Las aventuras, desventuras y sueños de Adonís García, el vampiro de la Colonia Roma*, 51; *En jirones*, 22, 53
Zayas de Lima, Perla: *Diccionario de autores teatrales argentinos*, 103